MODELING AND DESIGNING ACCOUNTING SYSTEMS

Using Access to Build a Database
First Edition

C. JANIE CHANG, PH.D.

San Jose State University

LAURA R. INGRAHAM, PH.D.

San Jose State University

JOHN WILEY & SONS, INC.

*We dedicate this book to Robbie, Dan, Casey, and Paul
and to Ted, Theresa, and Brenda.
We are eternally grateful to them for all they have provided us in this endeavor:
their hours of proofreading, their time sacrificed with us, their words of
encouragement to persevere, and their belief in our ultimate success.*

Executive Editor	*Christopher DeJohn*
Project Editor	*Ed Brislin*
Vice President and Publisher	*Susan Elbe*
Marketing Manager	*Amy Yarnevich*
Editorial Assistant	*Alison Stanley*
Production Manager	*Pamela Kennedy*
Senior Production Editor	*Sarah Wolfman-Robichaud*
Creative Director/Designer	*Harry Nolan*
Designer	*Hope Miller*
Illustrations Coordinator	*Mary Alma*
Senior Illustration Editor	*Anna Melhorn*
Senior Media Editor	*Allison Morris*
Copyeditor	*Kathy Drasky*
Project Manager	*Veena Kaul/Thomson Digital*
Cover Photo	*© Corbis Images*

This book was set in 10/12 Times Roman by Thomson Digital and printed and bound by
R.R. Donnelley-Crawfordsville. The cover was printed by Lehigh Press.

This book is printed on acid free paper.

TO THE STUDENT

More organizations today are turning from general ledger packages to database management systems to manage their accounting and other important operational data. In addition, increasingly, accounting systems are viewed in terms of enterprise-wide information systems which, by definition, are database management systems. These systems provide accountants and management with the information they need to make the important day-to-day decisions, control operations, and make strategic plans for the future.

Good database design methodology follows two approaches: the normalization approach or the semantic database modeling approach, better known as REA data modeling. This text follows the REA data modeling approach to designing and building databases. While this approach is software-independent, we will utilize *Microsoft Access 2003* to implement the data models throughout the text.

This book will provide you with an understanding of the theory of data modeling, as well as a practical application of those concepts and their ultimate implementation in database design. You will begin in Chapters 1 and 2 with the concepts of data modeling. Chapter 3 introduces the application of those concepts to database design using *Access*. Finally, in Chapters 4 through 6, you begin to build an actual system.

In Chapter 4, the Sales/Collection Business Process, you will develop your skills in building tables, forms, simple queries, and a basic report. Chapter 5, the Acquisition/Payment Business Process, explores complex queries, forms, and reports. Finally, in Chapter 6 (Human Resource Business Process), you create simple macros, imbed internal controls in table designs, and develop even more complex queries.

By actively working through the step-by-step instructions in these chapters, you will gain the experience of actually building an accounting information system. In addition, we have provided multiple choice and discussion questions for you, as well as additional problems, at the end of each chapter to reinforce your learning.

TO THE INSTRUCTOR

Accounting information systems has proven to be one of the more challenging courses to teach in the curriculum. There are several reasons for this. One is that there is no agreement as to how many courses are ideal in terms of coverage of the topic. Many schools offer a single course, others have two courses, and very few others offer a full major in the area of accounting information systems.

This book is intended to be a supplement to any text that is utilized in either an introductory AIS course or a database modeling and design course. It provides you with both a conceptual and a practical approach to data modeling from a resource-event-agent (REA) perspective and database design using *Microsoft Access 2003* as a platform. The first two chapters provide the fundamental concepts and theory for data modeling. Later chapters provide step-by-step detailed instructions for students to follow as they begin to model and design three essential processes of an accounting information system: the sales/collection process, the acquisition/payment process, and the human resources/payroll process. Working through these processes, students will have the opportunity to build tables, forms, queries, and reports. In addition, there are end-of-chapter multiple choice questions, discussion questions, and additional problems for students to work through once they have completed the chapter exercises. A CD-ROM containing the additional data and forms students will need to complete each chapter is included.

An electronic Instructor's Manual includes:

- Solutions Manual for all chapters
- Detailed lecture suggestions
- PowerPoint slides for Chapters 1–3

ABOUT THE AUTHORS

C. Janie Chang is a Professor of Accounting Information Systems (AIS) at San Jose State University (SJSU). She received her Ph.D. from the University of California, Irvine. Before moving to the Silicon Valley, Dr. Chang taught at California State University San Marcos and was elected as the Accounting Faculty of the Year for three consecutive years (1995–98). Since joining the faculty at SJSU, Dr. Chang was responsible for developing the undergraduate AIS program at SJSU. In addition, she assisted SJSU students in establishing the student chapter of Information Systems Audit and Control Association (ISACA) in 2002. Dr. Chang's current teaching responsibilities include AIS, Advanced AIS, IS Audit, Issues in E-Business, and Business Networks and Controls. Dr. Chang is very active and productive in research. Her studies have been published in leading academic journals including *Abacus, Auditing: A Journal of Practice and Theory, Behavioral Research in Accounting, Data Base, Journal of Accounting Literature,* etc. In 2003, Dr. Chang received the SJSU College of Business Outstanding Academic/Theoretical Research Award.

Laura R. Ingraham is an Associate Professor of Accounting Information Systems at San Jose State University. She holds both a Ph.D. in Business Administration and a Bachelor of Science in Accounting from Arizona State University. Prior to arriving at San Jose State, Dr. Ingraham served as an Assistant Professor at CSU San Marcos and at North Carolina State University State University, where she developed several distance education courses. Dr. Ingraham is the co-author of four textbooks and has written more than a dozen research papers on information systems, e-commerce, taxation, and accounting topics. Her work has been published in *Expert Systems with Applications, The CPA Journal, The New Review of Applied Expert Systems and Emerging Technologies, Strategic Finance, Tax Notes, Journal of State Taxation,* etc. Dr. Ingraham's current teaching responsibilities include Accounting Information Systems, Advanced AIS and Risk Management, and Issues in E-Business. She has also taught in the areas of taxation and introductory financial and managerial accounting. Dr. Ingraham is the recipient of the 2005 San Jose State University College of Business Outstanding Undergraduate Instructor Award.

ACKNOWLEDGMENTS

We worked collaboratively with many groups to bring this book to fruition. We want to thank the various anonymous reviewers and the following reviewers for their efforts and insightful comments: Liming Guan, University of Hawaii; Kathy Hurtt, Baylor University; Bonnie Klamm, North Dakota State University; Linda Parsons, George Mason University; and Rodney Smith, University of Arkansas.

We also want to thank our incredible publishing team at John Wiley & Sons, Inc. for their tireless and professional efforts in this endeavor: Christopher DeJohn, Executive Editor; Ed Brislin, Project Editor; Sarah Wolfman-Robichaud, Senior Production Editor; Alison Stanley, Editorial Assistant.

Finally, we would like to thank Jay O'Callaghan for his initial interest in and support of this project.

TRADEMARKS

Microsoft and Access are registered trademarks. Screen shots are reprinted by permission from Microsoft Corporation.

TABLE OF CONTENTS

CHAPTER 1

BUSINESS PROCESSES, DATA MODELING, AND INFORMATION SYSTEMS

INTRODUCTION

Despite the rapid growth in networks and information technology, many companies today are still using separate subsystems in their daily operations to support such specialized functions as marketing information systems, accounting information systems, personnel information systems, and so forth. When management professionals make decisions based on information obtained within one functional area, those decisions, which are apt to be made from a narrow perspective, may not be in the best interest of the company. Given the current business environment, companies should carefully examine every step in their business processes and question the necessity of each step. It is critical for companies to use the power of modern information technology such as enterprise resource planning (ERP) applications to improve company performance.

The database approach emphasizes the integration and sharing of data across major functional areas based on the company's business processes. This approach requires a fundamental reorientation or shift in business processes, starting with top management and affecting all employees. That is, the design of an information system is event-driven according to business processes. The purpose of this chapter is to start from the top and use data models to describe a company's business processes. Later chapters will use this business-process-based data modeling approach to assist you in learning how to design a relational database for a company. After completing this chapter, you should be able to:

- Identify resources, events, and agents (REA) in a data model
- Develop basic data models
- Recognize and evaluate the cardinalities in a data model
- Model a company's business processes using an REA diagram

BUSINESS PROCESSES AND DATA MODELING

Data modeling is the process of creating a logical representation of the structure of a database based on a company's business processes. Data modeling is the most important task in the development of an effective database that can provide useful information for decision making. A commonly used business data modeling technique is called the *entity-relationship diagram* (ERD). The ERD uses a graphical representation to identify and document various entities and the relationships between those entities. Three major components of an ERD are entity, relationship, and attribute. An entity is anything about

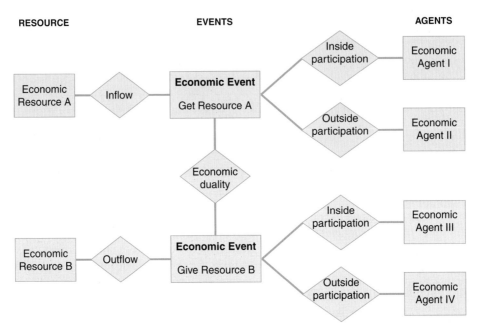

FIGURE 1-1 The REA Pattern
Adapted from McCarthy (1982).

which a company would like to collect and store information, such as "inventory," "purchase," and "vendor." A relationship is an association between entities, such as one or many inventory items included in each purchase transaction. An attribute is a characteristic of an entity, such as the inventory number and the description of each item in the entity of "inventory".[1] In an ERD, entities appear as rectangles, diamonds are used to represent relationships between entities, and small circles are used to show the attributes of each entity. Using ERD makes it relatively easy to understand a company's business processes and the relationships for those involved entities. ERD promotes communications between domain experts (such as accountants) and information technology (IT) professionals.

Based on the entity-relationship technique, the resource-event-agent (REA) data model is a framework specifically designed for building accounting information systems in a shared data environment.[2] First conceptualized by William E. McCarthy in 1982, it captures business processes by categorizing entities into economic resources, economic events, and economic agents. Resources are those things that have economic value to a company, such as cash and inventory. Events are the various business processes conducted in a company's daily operations, such as sales and purchases. Agents are the people and organizations, such as customers and salespeople, who participate in business events. Adapted from McCarthy (1982), Figure 1-1 shows the most basic REA pattern for modeling business processes. A general rule for creating REA diagrams is that each economic event should be linked to at least one economic resource and two economic agents.

---

[1]The concepts about attributes will be discussed in detail in the next chapter.

[2]McCarthy, W. E. 1982. The REA accounting model: A generalized framework for accounting systems in a shared data environment. *The Accounting Review* (July): 554–578.

The relationship shown between the two economic events in Figure 1-1 is referred to as an *economic duality relationship*. This is the causal relationship that occurs as a result of a give event (an economic decrement or an outflow) and a take event (an economic increment or an inflow). For example, in a revenue cycle, the give event could be sales (an outflow of inventory) and the take event could be cash receipts (an inflow of cash). In an expenditure cycle, the give event could be cash disbursements (an outflow of cash) and the take event could be purchases (an inflow of inventory).

REA MODELS AND TRANSACTION CYCLES

The database development process begins with enterprise modeling to set the range and general contents of organizational databases. This can be done effectively and efficiently by organizing an organization's subsystems around certain types of repetitive transactions. These groups of related transactions are called transaction cycles. Although different companies have different transactions, most companies have some transaction cycles in common: revenue, expenditure, human resource/payroll, and financing cycle. For manufacturing companies, the conversion/production cycle is another important component of their information systems.

Figure 1-2 shows the most basic economic events in the five transaction cycles. The revenue cycle includes the sale and cash receipt events. The expenditure cycle includes the

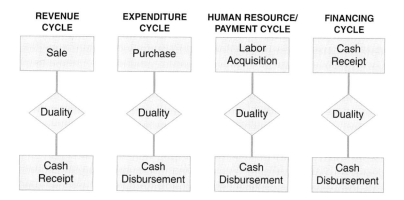

FIGURE 1-2 Basic Economic Events in Transaction Cycles

purchase and cash disbursement events. In addition, a company must acquire labor and pay wages/salaries through the human resources/payroll cycle. The financing cycle includes the events of obtaining funds from investors and/or creditors and paying them back. The conversion/production cycle includes events of using labor and machines to transform materials into finished goods.

The transaction cycles in Figure 1-2 are combined in Figure 1-3 into an REA model to create the entire accounting information system. This high-level conceptual model indicates how the transaction cycles interact with each other and with the financial reporting system.

Figure 1-4 provides sample REA diagrams for a revenue cycle and an expenditure cycle. In the expenditure cycle, a purchase transaction is made between a purchasing agent

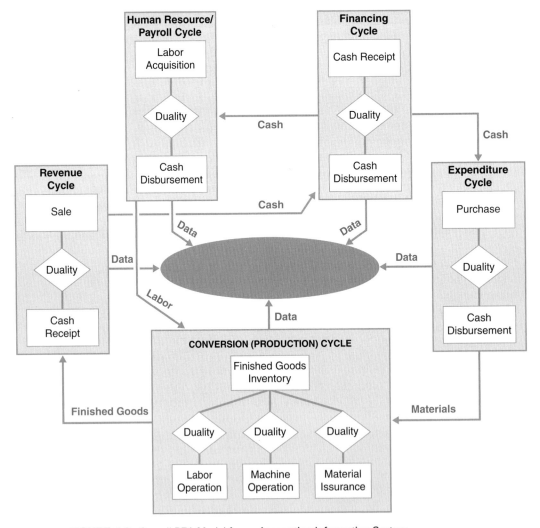

FIGURE 1-3   Overall REA Model for an Accounting Information System

Adapted from Romney, M. B. and P. J. Steinbart. 2006. *Accounting Information Systems.* 9th ed. Englewood Cliffs, N. J.: Prentice Hall, p. 30.

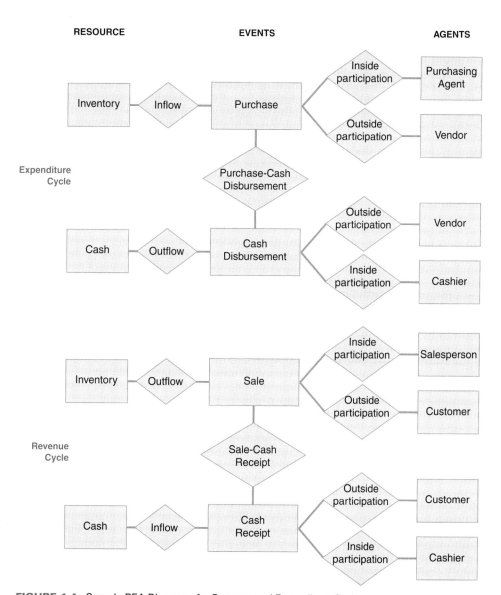

FIGURE 1-4   Sample REA Diagrams for Revenue and Expenditure Cycles

and a vendor and will increase inventory stocks. The purchase transaction will be paid by using cash involving the vendor and cashier in a cash disbursement event. In the revenue cycle, each sale transaction will decrease inventory, and a salesperson and a customer will participate in the transaction. Note that as we design the system that models these transactions, each entity needs to be shown only once. That is, there is just one "vendor" entity and one "customer" entity shown on Figure 1-4 despite the fact that the company has many vendors and customers. The sales transaction will be paid by receiving cash involving the participation of the customer and the cashier in a cash receipt event.

CARDINALITIES OF RELATIONSHIPS

Identification of relationships is a very important step in data modeling. A relationship establishes a logical connection between entities. Relationship examples in generic settings include: (1) Eric majors in finance; (2) Ben owns vehicle#104; and (3) Professor John Lewis teaches marketing (see Figure 1-5).

For data modeling purposes, Figure 1-6 provides corresponding diagrams to describe the three relationships.

Note that identifying entities and adding relationships to the diagrams are still insufficient in terms of describing how an entity participates in a specific relationship. For example, we should indicate that each student may major in one or more fields. One person may own zero vehicles, one vehicle, or many vehicles. The number of instances one entity can be linked to one specific instance of another entity is defined as a cardinality. With the information of cardinality at both ends of each relationship, we can easily understand the participation of each entity in the relationships. That is, cardinality information restricts the number of participation constraints in a relationship. In this book, cardinality is denoted as (*min,max*) where *min* is the minimum number and *max* is the maximum number that can participate in a relationship. What is the correct set of cardinalities in each relationship? Does each entity have a fixed set of cardinalities for all the relationships? The answer depends on the problem domain that you need to model. Regarding the person-vehicle example above, assume that Ben, Emily, and Tina own vehicle#104, vehicle#101 and vehicle#105, and vehicle#107, respectively. In addition, Michael does not own any vehicles. We can use the graphical representation in Figure 1-7 to show the relationship and cardinalities.

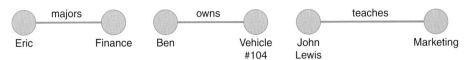

FIGURE 1-5 Sample Relationship Representation

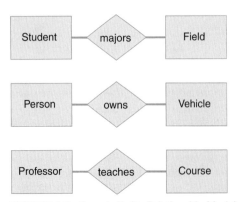

FIGURE 1-6 Sample Entity-Relationship Models

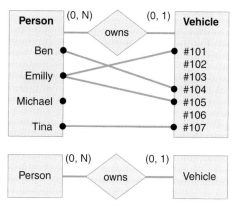

FIGURE 1-7 Person-Vehicle Example

In Figure 1-7, Emily owns two vehicles. Michael does not own any vehicles. Each of the other two people owns one vehicle. Thus, the cardinalities in this specific "person owns vehicle" relationship is (0,N) near the person entity, which means each person can own at least zero vehicles and at most many vehicles. "N" here means many. The cardinalities of (0,1) near the vehicle entity indicate that each vehicle may not be owned by a person yet. In addition, at most, each vehicle can be owned by one person only.[3]

Another example is the professor-course relationship. Figure 1-8 indicates that each professor teaches at least one course and may teach many courses. Different professors can

[3]This book uses Chen's notation for cardinalities. There are other commonly used notations: Crow's Foot and HDC. The following comparison is adapted from Dunn, C. L., J. W. Cherrington, and A. S. Hollander, 2005, *Enterprise Information Systems*, New York: McGraw-Hill, p. 59.

	Notation for each cardinality	Diagram format to the person-vehicle example
Chen (used in this textbook)	Min zero = (0, Min one = (1, Max one = ,1) Max many = ,N)	Person (0, N) owns (0, 1) Vehicle
Crow's Foot	Min zero = Min one = Max one = Max many =	Person Vehicle
HDC	Min zero = (0, Min one = (1, Max one = ,1) Max many = ,*)	Person (0, 1) (0, *) Vehicle

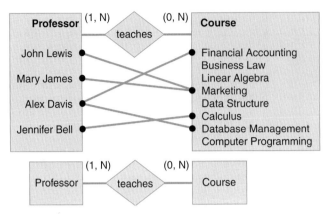

FIGURE 1-8   Professor-Course Example

FIGURE 1-9   Professor-Course-Student Example

teach the same course for different sessions. In addition, not all courses are taught every semester. In this example, professors John Lewis and Mary James both teach the marketing course, and business law is not taught by any professor in the current semester. For this type of relationship, we employ (1,N) near the "Professor" entity to represent that each professor teaches at least one and at most many courses. We employ (0,N) near the "Course" entity to show that each course can be taught by at least zero or at most many professors.

We may also add another entity called "Student," as well as its relationship, "Course is studied by Student," to the diagram (see Figure 1-9). This time, we will assume all students are full-time. We want to impose the restriction that each student must take at least 3 courses but no more than 6 courses in a semester. Accordingly, the cardinalities (0,N) and (3,6) are added to the diagram.

USING REA TO MODEL BUSINESS PROCESSES

There are three basic steps to construct an REA diagram to depict a company's business processes. After the business processes are modeled, the REA diagram should be validated by the company's experts who are knowledgeable about the details and objectives of the business processes. The three steps in developing an REA diagram are as follows:

1. Identify economic exchange events.
2. Identify the resources affected by each economic event and the agents who participate in those events.
3. Determine the cardinalities of each relationship.

The following section provides an example that demonstrates how to use the REA to model a small company's business processes.

Cherokee Art and Antique Store

Background   The Cherokee Art and Antique Store sells original art and antique pieces. Its owner, Jesse Lewis, started the store in 1990 in a small town with a rich Native-American culture. Jesse carries original paintings, crafts, jewelry, and special antiques from local Native-American artists and antique sellers. Jesse runs his business as a consignment store. First, he and the artists/sellers agree on a minimum price for the art/antique item. Then, Jesse sets a sale price and he takes a percentage of the sale price as his commission. He displays all the available pieces in the store. So far, Jesse has carried only original pieces of art and craft and antiques—no two are the same. Jesse has no employees to help him. Jesse takes care of all the selecting, buying, and selling himself.

Cherokee's Revenue Cycle   All sales occur in the store. Sales to customers consist of one or more pieces of art and/or the antiques displayed in the store. Other than cash and checks, Jesse accepts credit cards for sales. However, he requires that all customers pay in full for each transaction. Jesse goes to the bank every day to deposit daily cash receipts. Although Jesse has a couple of bank accounts for the Cherokee Art and Antique Store, he always deposits his daily revenue into the general checking account.

Model the Revenue Cycle Using REA   **To model business processes in the** <u>**revenue**</u> **cycle for the Cherokee Art and Antique Store (Cherokee), we first need to identify economic exchange events in the cycle.** Recall that in Figure 1-2 there are two basic events for any revenue cycle: "Sales" and "Cash Receipt." According to the descriptions stated in the previous paragraph, we can determine that these two events are proper for Cherokee. Therefore, the partial REA diagram in Figure 1-10 can be drawn.

The second step is to identify the resources affected by each economic event and the agents who participate in those events. For the "Sales" event, inventories of art and antiques are reduced and the participating agents are a customer and Jesse. For the "Cash Receipt" event, Jesse receives cash/checks from the customer. Accordingly, the REA in Figure 1-11 provides the basic business model for Cherokee's revenue cycle.

FIGURE 1-10   Sales-Cash Receipt Relationship

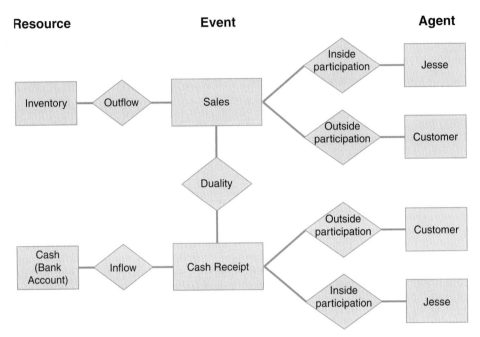

FIGURE 1-11 Basic REA Diagram for Cherokee's Revenue Cycle

The next step is to determine the cardinalities of each relationship. First, notice in Figure 1-12 that "Bank Account" is added to the resource "Cash," because this describes where the inflow of cash is recorded. According to the description of Cherokee's cash collection processes, the relationship between "Bank Account" and "Cash Receipt" should be (1,N) and (1,1). That is, a bank account will have at least one cash receipt deposit but can have many deposits. Each cash receipt is deposited into one, and only one, bank account.

Figure 1-13 indicates that the relationship between "Inventory" and "Sales" is (0,1) and (1,N). Each art piece or antique may not be sold yet; if it is sold, it can be sold once only, since all are originals. Hence, the minimum cardinality is zero and maximum cardinality is one for the "Inventory" entity. For each sale transaction, at least one piece of inventory and,

FIGURE 1-12 Cash-Cash Reciept Relationship

FIGURE 1-13 Inventory-Sales Relationship

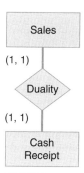

FIGURE 1-14 Sales-Cash Receipt Relationship

at most, many pieces of inventory can be sold. Hence, for the "Sales" entity, the minimum cardinality is one, and the maximum cardinality is many.

In Figure 1-14, we see that the relationship between "Sales" and "Cash Receipt" is (1,1) and (1,1). Each sale transaction has one, and only one, cash receipt, and each cash receipt event is for one sale transaction only. All customers must pay in full at the time when the transaction occurs, although Jesse accepts credit cards. In other words, there are no accounts receivable and no partial payments, so the cardinalities are (1,1) at the "Sales" side. In addition, at the "Cash Receipt" side, each cash receipt relates to one transaction only since the customers must pay at the time of sale.

If Cherokee bills customers periodically (for a few transactions), then the cardinalities would be (1,N) at the "Cash Receipt" side as indicated in Figure 1-15. In that case, each cash receipt would be related to many sales transactions. Due to the fact that customers could delay payments (i.e., monthly billing), Cherokee would have accounts receivables. This would result in a scenario of **accounts receivable** as indicated by the **zero** minimum cardinality at the "Sales" side. If customers still must pay in full, the maximum cardinality at the "Sales" side is one.

Figure 1-16 provides the complete REA diagram for Cherokee's revenue cycle. In terms of the cardinalities between events and agents, the general case is (1,1) at the event side and (1,N) at the agent side. Each sale transaction relates to one customer only, and each customer can participate in many sale transactions. Here, the internal agent, Jesse, is

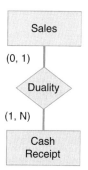

FIGURE 1-15 Sales-Cash Receipt Relationship (with Accounts Receivable)

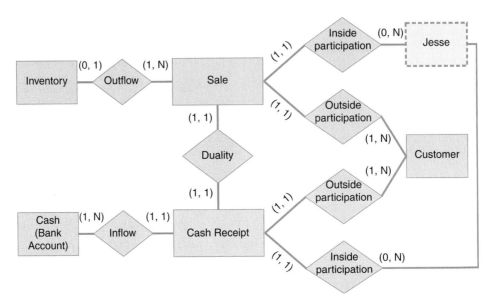

FIGURE 1-16 Complete REA Diagram for Cherokee's Revenue Cycle

denoted in a dotted-line box that means he is the only person conducting the sale transactions; thus, we do *not* need to track information about him. In addition, in the REA diagram, we need to illustrate each entity only once. Therefore, we do not need to show two rectangles for the "Customer" entity and "Jesse."

Cherokee's Expenditure Cycle Jesse does not pay the artist or seller of antiques until he sells the piece. Most of the artists and sellers know him very well and are willing to wait for Jesse to sell their pieces. In general, Jesse pays them once each week for the sales made that week. Each purchase may include several items from a single artist. Jesse always writes a check to pay each artist or seller when he successfully sells the art and/or antique piece(s).

Model the Expenditure Cycle Using REA **To model business processes in the <u>expenditure</u> cycle for Cherokee, we first identify economic exchange events in the cycle.** Recall that in Figure 1-2 there are two basic events for any expenditure cycle: "Purchase" and "Cash Disbursement." According to the descriptions stated in the previous paragraph, we can see that these two events are proper for Cherokee. Therefore, the partial REA diagram in Figure 1-17 can be drawn.

    The second step is to identify the resources affected by each economic event and the agents who participate in those events. For the "Purchase" event, inventories of art and antiques are purchased, and the participating agents are the artist/seller and Jesse. For the "Cash Disbursement" event, Jesse pays each artist/seller in full after he sells the inventory. The REA diagram in Figure 1-18 shows the basic business model for Cherokee's expenditure cycle.

FIGURE 1-17   Purchase-Cash Disbursement Relationship

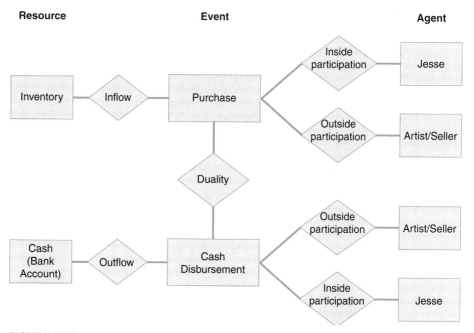

FIGURE 1-18   Basic REA Diagram for Cherokee's Expenditure Cycle

The next step is to determine the cardinalities of each relationship. Since Cherokee's checks are written from one account only, and at least one and at most many checks can be written from the bank account, the relationship between "Bank Account" and "Cash Disbursement" should be (1,N) and (1,1) as indicated in Figure 1-19.

Figure 1-20 shows us that the relationship between "Inventory" and "Purchase" is (1,1) and (1,N). That is, each art and antique piece is purchased once and once only. For each purchase transaction, at least one piece of inventory and at most many pieces of inventory can be bought.

The relationship between "Purchase" and "Cash Disbursement" is (0,N) and (1,N) as shown in Figure 1-21. In other words, Jesse does not pay at the time of purchase. This is the zero at the "Purchase" side, which shows that there are accounts payable. He pays the artist

FIGURE 1-19   Cash-Cash Disbursement Relationship

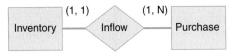

FIGURE 1-20   Inventory-Purchase Relationship

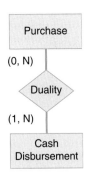

FIGURE 1-21   Purchase-Cash Disbursement Relationship

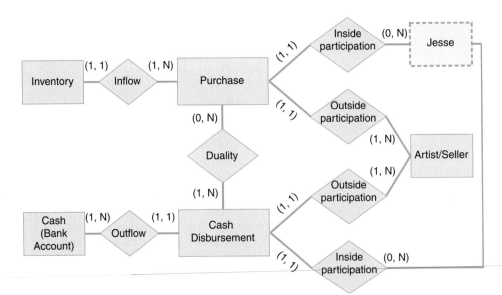

FIGURE 1-22   Complete REA Diagram for Cherokee's Expenditure Cycle

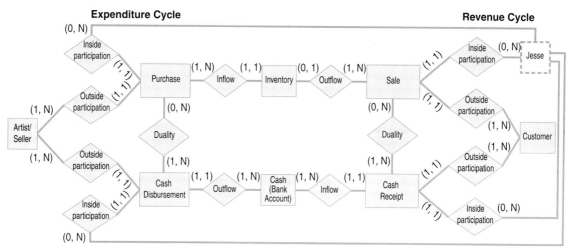

FIGURE 1-23 Comprehensive REA Data Model for Cherokee Art and Antique Store

after an item is sold. Each purchase may not be paid in full, since items purchased from the vendors in one transaction may not have all been sold at the same time. This is why the maximum cardinality at the "Purchase" side is many (N). Each cash disbursement (i.e., a check) can be for one purchase or for many purchases since Jesse pays each artist or seller once per week.

In terms of the cardinalities between events and agents, as mentioned in the revenue cycle, the general case is (1,1) at the event side and (1,N) at the agent side. In addition, in an REA diagram, we need to illustrate each entity once only. Figure 1-22 shows the completed REA diagram for Cherokee's expenditure cycle.

Finally, to make a comprehensive data model for Cherokee, we combine the revenue and expenditure cycle processes as illustrated in the REA diagram in Figure 1-23.

KEY TERMS

entity	duality	economic events
relationship	entity-relationship diagram (ERD)	economic agents
cardinality	REA data model	
data modeling	economic resources	

QUESTIONS AND PROBLEMS FOR REVIEW

MULTIPLE-CHOICE QUESTIONS

1.1 Which of the following is considered an entity in an REA data model?
(a) Customer
(b) Sale
(c) Finished goods
(d) All of the above are correct.

1.2 A construction company always let its customers make installment payments. When the company signs a contract with a customer, the customer is required to pay one percent of the total price as down payment. So far, no customer has paid in full at once. Which set of cardinality correctly shows this relationship?

(a) Sales (0,1) − (1,N) Cash receipts

(b) Sales (1,1) − (1,N) Cash receipts

(c) Sales (0,N) − (1,1) Cash receipts

(d) Sales (1,N) − (1,1) Cash receipts

1.3 A construction company only builds custom homes. So far, none of its customers has ordered two houses at one time. Which set of cardinality correctly shows the relationship between inventory and sales?

(a) Inventory (0,1) − (1,1) Sales

(b) Inventory (1,1) − (1,1) Sales

(c) Inventory (1,1) − (1,N) Sales

(d) Inventory (0,N) − (0,1) Sales

1.4 A grocery store accepts cash, checks, and credit card payments from customers. Which set of cardinality correctly shows the relationship between sales and cash receipts?

(a) Sales (0,1) − (0,1) Cash receipts

(b) Sales (1,1) − (0,1) Cash receipts

(c) Sales (1,1) − (1,1) Cash receipts

(d) Sales (1,N) − (1,1) Cash receipts

1.5 A large company with several business lines has different types of bank accounts with a few banks. Each business line has its own checking account for cash disbursements and cash receipts. Which set of cardinality correctly shows the relationship between cash (bank accounts) and cash disbursements for the company (not for each business line)?

(a) Cash (0,N) − (0,1) Cash disbursements

(b) Cash (0,N) − (1,1) Cash disbursements

(c) Cash (1,1) − (1,N) Cash disbursements

(d) Cash (1,N) − (1,N) Cash disbursements

1.6 A traditional book store just started its e-business using a Web site to take customer orders. Which set of cardinality correctly shows the relationship between sales and salespeople?

(a) Sales (0,1) − (0,1) Salespeople

(b) Sales (0,1) − (1,1) Salespeople

(c) Sales (0,1) − (0,N) Salespeople

(d) Sales (1,1) − (1,N) Salespeople

1.7 A real estate company has many agents buying and selling residential properties and business sites. The company has quite high turnover rates of these agents. Which set of cardinality correctly shows the relationship between sales and agents?

(a) Sales (0,1) − (0,1) Agents

(b) Sales (1,1) − (0,1) Agents

(c) Sales (1,1) − (0,N) Agents

(d) Sales (1,1) − (1,N) Agents

1.8 A retail company would like to store information about current and potential vendors who supply inventories to the company. Which set of cardinality correctly shows this relationship?

(a) Inventory (1,1) − (0,N) Vendor

(b) Inventory (1,N) − (1,N) Vendor

(c) Inventory (1,N) – (0,N) Vendor

(d) Inventory (1,N) – (1,1) Vendor

1.9 Which one of the following statements about the REA data model is true?

(a) Each resource is generally linked to at least two agents.

(b) Each event is generally linked to at least three agents.

(c) Each event is generally linked to at least one resource.

(d) Each agent is generally linked to at least two events.

PROBLEMS

1.1 Cherokee Art and Antique Store

Develop an REA diagram for Cherokee Art and Antique Store's expenditure cycle to model its purchasing and payment events related to artists/sellers given the following new fact that Jesse likes to collect information on potential artists/sellers for future business. Other situations remain the same.

1.2 Cherokee Art and Antique Store

Develop an REA diagram for Cherokee Art and Antique Store's acquisition activities to model its expenditures related to the purchasing of store furniture, office equipment, and other fixed assets only. Assume that Jesse always makes installment payments for asset acquisition. He writes a check for the payment of each asset even if several assets have been purchased from the same vendor, since this way is easier for him to track the unpaid balance of each item. Occasionally, a vendor does *not* require a down payment.

1.3 Cherokee Art and Antique Store

Develop an REA diagram for Cherokee Art and Antique Store's expenditure cycle to model its purchasing and payment events in general (not to include the acquisition event in Problem 1.2). That is, not only buying art pieces and paying the artists, Cherokee also buys office supplies, orders services for maintenance, and pays for other operating expenses such as water and utilities, telephone, and cleaning.

1.4 Velvet Lounge

Background: Velvet Lounge is a premier upscale nightclub located in the heart of San Francisco. It has two levels, which are fully stocked with two bars on each level. Velvet Lounge is richly decorated with velvet furniture, mahogany walls, and giant chandeliers to create a very luxurious setting.

Velvet Lounge may be entirely rented for hosting a private event. Most of the time, the club is rented out for people to host a theme party or an after-party for concerts or other special events. People who tend to rent the entire club are mostly promoters or radio stations. Admission fees are to be determined by the host of the event and all of the admission fees go to the host. This gives the promoters an incentive to bring in a large crowd.

Velvet Lounge has private VIP rooms that may be rented for birthday parties and special occasions on a smaller scale. Depending on the size of the room that is rented, the customer will be given a certain number of VIP guest passes.

Internet Use: Velvet Lounge's official Web site enables customers to see upcoming events at the club. The Web site is used to provide background information about the club to the public. General information such as location and management contact information is posted on the site. Pictures of the club are also posted on the site.

Velvet Lounge's Web site allows customers to subscribe to its mailing list and to be notified of special events. This allows Velvet Lounge to keep in touch with its customer base. The mailing list is also a great tool for targeted promotions.

Detailed information about VIP room rentals is available from the Web site. Customers may submit a request to reserve a VIP room or the entire club through the Internet with their contact information. Each request is assigned to a manager who will then check for availability and respond to the customer.

Expenditure Cycle: Velvet Lounge purchases alcohol and other beverages from several vendors. The vendors provide different products or only one product for the club. Once Velvet Lounge has ordered from a vendor, the vendor remains in the database even if the club has not made any recent purchases from the vendor. A purchase can consist of multiple beverage items or it can include only one kind of beverage. All purchase orders must be made by the purchasing manager. Depending on the payment terms with specific vendors, Velvet's payments may be due in full upon delivery or payments may be due within 30 days of receipt of goods. Either way only one check is issued per purchase order because payments are always made in full. Only the cashier is authorized to handle cash disbursements and cash receipts. Velvet Lounge uses a single checking account for cash disbursements and cash receipts. All inventories are stored on-site in the stockroom of the club.

Revenue Cycle: Velvet Lounge has two sources of income: room rentals and bar service. A customer can rent the entire club or the VIP rooms. Velvet Lounge does not distinguish between the two different customer bases. All rental reservations are initiated by the request of a customer in person or via the telephone, fax, or the Internet. Once a reservation request has been received it is directed to a manager for approval. The manager assigned to the specific reservation request will check the company database for availability and respond to the customer accordingly. If the room is available, the manager will provide a quote for the customer. When the customer confirms reservation of the room(s), all the necessary contact information of the customer is entered into the database. Payment in full for the rental is due upon confirmation of the reservation. That is, Velvet Lounge receives one payment for every rental reservation.

Velvet Lounge also serves drinks from its bars. Velvet Lounge has full control of all the bars and retains all of its proceeds. Only staff employees take drink orders and serve the drinks. Velvet Lounge employees serve at the bar and the VIP rooms. Similarly, all orders must be paid for in full at the time of purchase. Again, cashiers are the only employees who handle all the cash receipts from room rentals and drinks purchases.

Required:

1. Construct an REA diagram to depict Velvet Lounge's revenue cycle.

2. Construct an REA diagram to depict Velvet Lounge's expenditure cycle.

1.5 Worifree Properties, Inc.

Background: Worifree Properties is a small start-up company that came into existence in the spring of 2005 with a total of six employees. Headquartered in San Jose, California, the company has experienced moderate growth in its first year. Its core business focuses on property management. Worifree performs all property management-related tasks to satisfy the needs of its clients. Its clients are real estate investors/owners who are interested in renting out their property without incurring the work and worry associated with its management. Worifree attempts to reduce owner involvement in the management process as much as possible while providing property owners with accurate and reliable services and accounting.

Worifree's clients own one or more properties in the Bay Area. Although a property may have more than one owner, most multiple owners are married couples. In those cases, Worifree keeps track of only one of the owners. Worifree performs rent collection, maintenance, and advertising, and prepares contracts on behalf of the property owners for leasing transactions. Maintenance and advertising services are all outsourced to contractors, while lease handling and other services are managed by internal employees. All cash inflows and outflows are controlled through one bank account, although Worifree has a couple of different bank accounts with the same bank. In addition, because the company has so few employees, many transactions are handled online via electronic funds transfers. For example, Worifree agrees to electronically forward the rental income to corresponding owners immediately upon receiving them from the tenant(s). All tenants are required to make rental payments to Worifree using electronic funds transfers.

Revenue Cycle: Worifree's revenue is from one source only—property owners. A revenue transaction is recorded strictly for services performed by Worifree's employees or its contractors on one property. Contractor services include those for maintenance and advertising on clients' properties. The contractors invoice Worifree for services performed on a particular occasion that may include one or more services. Once the contractors are paid, Worifree, in turn, invoices the property owner with a service invoice for the expenditures. Worifree invoices its clients for the same amount as the contractors invoice Worifree.

Included in Worifree's service invoice is a monthly property management fee and charges for other services performed by its employees, such as new rental lease arrangements and maintenance expenditures. An invoice involves only one employee, but an employee can handle more than one invoice. Service invoices are prepared for each client every month and the client is required to pay in full for each bill. On rare occasions, some clients may not pay on time and Worifree accepts late payments with financial charges. Worifree maintains only current clients' information in its database. The cash collections are done through electronic funds transfer; thus, no employee is involved in the cash collection process.

Expenditure Cycle: The expenditure cycle of Worifree is not complex. There are two kinds of expenditures: (1) services provided by contractors and (2) supplies/fixed assets purchased from vendors. Maintenance and advertising services are provided by a specified set of vendors for quality and cost control. Since Worifree always gets services from contractors with whom they have had transactions before, there could be a delay to get the desired service when certain contractors are busy. Some contractors provide more than one kind of service for Worifree. When each service is completed and Worifree is billed, Worifree always pays the contractor electronically in full.

When making purchases, Worifree uses a specified set of qualified vendors. Some vendors in the vendor list are alternate vendors. Worifree orders from the alternate vendors only if the often-used vendor does not have a specific item in stock. All purchases are made by purchasing agents. Each purchase involves only one purchasing agent and one vendor. Vendors may provide Worifree with one or more than one type of product on more than one occasion. Payments for most purchases are made in full. Some vendors bill Worifree monthly, particularly for office supplies. However, when purchasing expensive office equipment or large furniture, Worifree makes installment payments. Since Worifree has an excellent credit history, some vendors do not require a down payment for installment purchases.

Required:

1. Construct an REA diagram to depict Worifree's revenue cycle.
2. Construct an REA diagram to depict Worifree's expenditure cycle.

CHAPTER 2

DATA MODELS AND RELATIONAL DATABASES

INTRODUCTION

The database development process begins with **enterprise modeling** to set the range and general contents of organizational databases as presented in Chapter 1. The example of an enterprise model is reproduced in Figure 2-1 for a review.

Then, in the **conceptual data modeling stage**, the requirements of overall entities are analyzed based on transaction cycles. For example, Figure 2-2 is a conceptual data model for Cherokee's revenue and expenditure cycles as discussed in Chapter 1.

This chapter concerns **logical database design**. Logical database design is the process of transforming the conceptual data model into a logical data model. The logical data models used in this chapter are relational data models. Most information systems today are based on relational databases, the most popular type of databases used for transaction processing.

The purpose of this chapter is to expand on our discussion in Chapter 1 using business-process-based data models to design a relational database. This chapter presents important concepts and definitions of relational databases. In addition, the processes of normalization that determine whether a table is well designed and eliminate possible anomalies in the table are also discussed. After completing this chapter, you should be able, based on a data model, to accomplish the following:

- Identify primary and foreign keys for each entity and relationship in the data model
- Create tables that are linked properly with foreign keys or through relationship table(s)
- Examine whether a table design has any anomalies
- Normalize a table to third normal form

RELATIONAL DATABASES

Basic Concepts and Definitions

A database is an organized collection of logically related data[4] that are stored in tables (or files). There are three main constructs of the structure of a relational database. The primary construct is called a **relation** or a **table**, that is a storage structure with rows and

---

[4]Data are facts, text, and images that can be recorded and stored on computer media, such as customer names, logos, and addresses. Information is data that has been processed and organized in such a way that it can increase the knowledge of decision makers, such as a report with the due date and accounts receivable balance of each customer.

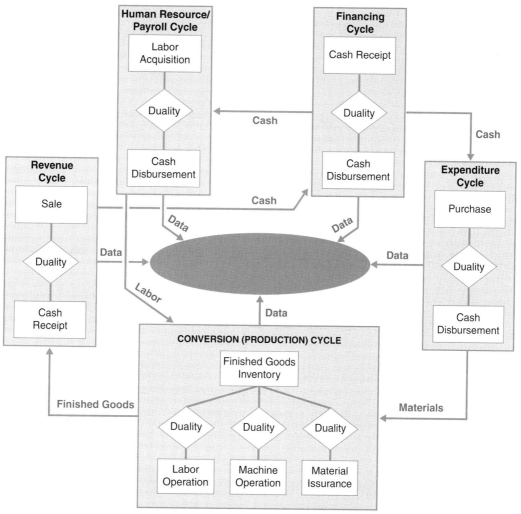

FIGURE 2-1 Overall REA Model for an Accounting Information System

Adapted from Romney, M. B. and P. J. Steinbart. 2006. *Accounting Information Systems.* 9th ed. Englewood Cliffs, N. J.: Prentice Hall, p. 30.

columns much like a spreadsheet. Each table in a database represents either an entity or a relationship between entities. Tables need to be properly linked to one another to make a relational database. The **columns** in a table are called **fields** and represent the **attributes** or characteristics of the entity or relationship. The **rows** in a table are called **records** or **tuples.** The records represent all the specific data values that are associated with one instance.

In Chapter 1, using an REA diagram, we created the data model for Cherokee's revenue cycle. This data model is repeated in Figure 2-3.

When we convert an REA diagram to a database, each entity becomes a table, which is a storage structure with rows and columns much like a spreadsheet. Therefore, according to Figure 2-3, Cherokee's revenue cycle database consists of the following five tables: Inventory Table, Cash Table, Sale Table, Cash Receipt Table, and Customer Table. Recall

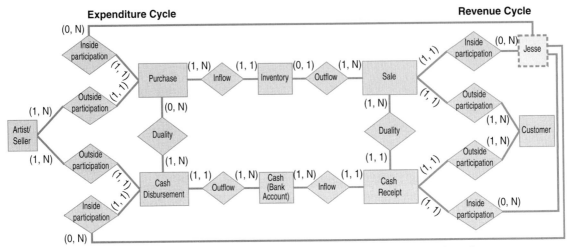

FIGURE 2-2   Comprehensive REA Data Model for Cherokee Art and Antique Store

from Chapter 1 that we do not need to track information about Jesse since he is the only person conducting sales. Therefore, it is not necessary to have a table to store data about Jesse. If there were more than one salesperson, this would be necessary. In general, however, we need to create a table for each entity in the REA diagram to store data important to the company.

Each column of a table represents an attribute (or characteristic) of its entity. For example, the attributes for the Customer Table may include Customer ID, Customer Name,

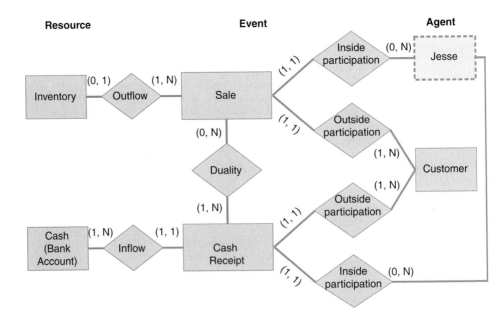

FIGURE 2-3   Complete REA Diagram for Cherokee's Revenue Cycle

Customer Address, Customer City, Customer State, Customer ZIP Code, and Customer Phone Number and Customer Email. Each row of a table represents an instance (or a record) of the entity. That is, one specific row in the Customer Table provides all the data values for one specific customer. A **primary key** attribute is a **unique** identifier of each instance of an entity. For example, the primary key of the Customer Table is Customer ID. Customer Name would not be an appropriate primary key unless Jesse is *absolutely* sure that he does not and will not ever have customers with the same name, which is a practical impossibility.

An important property of the relational database is that it represents relationships between entities by including values stored in the columns of the corresponding tables. For example, the Cash Receipt Table may include attributes such as Cash Receipt #, Date, Amount, and Customer ID. By including the Customer ID in the Cash Receipt Table we can link the Cash Receipt Table and the Customer Table to obtain data for decision-making purposes. For example, we can easily link a cash receipt to its associated customer.

The Customer ID is called a **foreign key** in the Cash Receipt Table. A foreign key is an attribute appearing in one table that is a primary key in another table. Foreign keys are used to link tables. Another example of using a foreign key would be including "Item #" as an attribute in the Sale Table. "Item #" in the Sale Table then would be a foreign key because (assuming continuity of table design) it is the primary key of the Inventory Table.

We can use the cardinalities in the REA diagram from Chapter 1 to determine these relationships between the entities in terms of a relational database. We do this by referring to the maximum cardinality on each side of the relation in the REA diagram. Since we know that a maximum cardinality can be a 1 or an N, we have three possible relationships. A one-to-one (1:1) relationship occurs when a record (row) in a table relates to a record in another table once and only once. A one-to-many (1:N) relationship occurs when a record in a table can relate to several records in another table. A many-to-many (N:N) relationship occurs when several records in a table relate to several records in another table.

Basic Requirements of Tables

The relational database approach imposes some requirements on the structure of tables. If these basic requirements are not fulfilled or if data redundancy exists in a database, problems (called anomalies) may occur. The requirements include the following:

- **The Entity Integrity Rule:** Each table in a relational database must have a primary key attribute, and it must have a value for each record (i.e., it cannot be null).
- **The Referential Integrity Rule:** We use foreign keys to link tables so the corresponding values must match. A value for a foreign key attribute must either be null or match one of the data values that correspond to the value of a primary key attribute in another table.
- **Each attribute must be uniquely named**
- Values of a specific attribute must be of the same type. In other words, a column must be designated as text, numeric, currency, etc., and the data must be of only that type. For example, data in a column designated as currency must all be in dollars and cents format.
- Each attribute (column) of a record (row) must be **single-valued.** This requirement forces us to create a relationship table for each many-to-many relationship.

FIGURE 2-4 Inventory-Sales Relationship

For example, for a grocery store, the relationship between the entities of "inventory" and "sale" is often a many-to-many relationship, as indicated in Figure 2-4. That is, each kind of inventory could be sold many times. And, the store may sell different kinds of inventory in one transaction. If we include the attribute of "Item #" in the Sale Table as a foreign key so that we know which items are sold, each sale record may have **several** values for the attribute of "Item #," which violates the requirement that each attribute of a record must be single-valued. A similar problem occurs when we try to use "Sale #" as a foreign key in the Inventory Table. Therefore, we must create an additional table, a relationship table, to link two tables with a many-to-many relationship. In Figure 2-4, the relationship table is called the Line Item Table (in the diamond-shaped relationship symbol). This Line Item Table is used to link the Inventory Table and the Sales Table. Recall that each sale may include many kinds of inventory items. The primary key[5] of this Line Item table is a two-column attribute that includes both Sale # and Item # to make each record unique, and to link the Inventory Table and the Sales Table. An example in Microsoft Access is shown in Figure 2-5. The symbol of "∞" in Access means many.

- All other attributes (columns) in a table must describe a characteristic of the entity identified by the primary key. For example, including customer address or phone number as an attribute in the Cash Receipt Table would be incorrect. To link to this

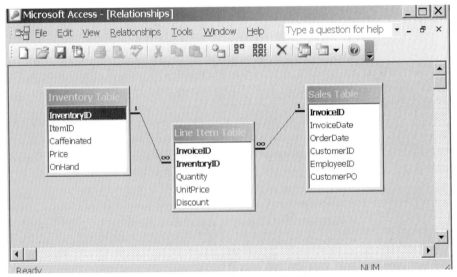

FIGURE 2-5 Inventory-Sales Relationship Depicted in ACCESS

---

[5] The primary key in a relationship table is always a combined key, composed of the primary keys from tables in the relationship. This is called a concatenated primary key and may also be called a composite key.

information, you would include Customer ID in the table as a foreign key but since neither customer address nor phone number is a characteristic of the cash receipt event, they must not be included in the Cash Receipt Table.

The sequence of attributes or records in a table is of no importance.

Steps of Implementing an REA Diagram in a Relational Database

We will use the same example in Chapter 1, Cherokee Art and Antique Store, to illustrate how to implement an REA diagram in a relational database.

Step 1:   Create a table for each entity.
According to Cherokee's REA data model in Figure 2-2, we need to create the following eight tables for the entities: Inventory Table, Cash Table, Sale Table, Cash Receipt Table, Purchase Table, Cash Disbursement Table, Artist Table, and Customer Table. Note that the title of each table should be the same as the name of the entity it represents, so it is easy to refer back to the original data model design.

Step 2:   Create a table for each many-to-many relationship.
One relationship table is needed for the many-to-many relationship between the events of "Purchase" and "Cash Disbursement" (i.e., Duality 1). To make it easy to understand, we name this relationship table Purchase-Cash Disbursement. In addition, the name of the relationship on the REA diagram should also be renamed as Purchase-Cash Disbursement.

Step 3:   Examine tables with a one-to-one relationship.
We need to examine the entities with a one-to-one relationship carefully because they often should be collapsed into one entity. Since all sales are paid for immediately in cash, Cherokee has a one-to-one relationship between the events "Sales" and "Cash Receipt." The sales data Cherokee might need would include a primary key (e.g., sales invoice number), sales date (which would be the same as cash receipt date), dollar amount, and type of payment such as cash, check, or credit card. Therefore, we can collapse the two tables into one table called Sales Table. When such a decision has been made, Cherokee's REA model should be modified accordingly.

Step 4:   Identify the attributes and assign the primary key for each table.
There are several ways to present a table structure. The table structure adopted here is a simple form in which a table's attributes are enclosed in parentheses following the table name and a double underline indicates the primary key column(s).[6] Based on Cherokee's REA data model, its table structures are listed as follows:

Inventory Table (Item #, Inventory Description, Inventory Cost)

Cash Table (Account #, Account Type, Balance)

Sales Table (Sale #, Sale Date, Sale Amount, Payment Type)

---

[6]There are other conventions for indicating keys. For example, a primary key and a foreign key could be identified using a single underline and an asterisk, respectively.

Purchase Table (<u>Purchase #</u>, Purchase Date, Purchase Amount)

Cash Disbursement Table (<u>Check #</u>, Check Date, Payment Amount)

Artist Table (<u>Artist ID</u>, Artist Name, Artist Address, Artist phone #, Artist Email)

Customer Table (<u>Customer ID</u>, Customer Name, Customer Address, Customer
City, Customer State, Customer ZIP Code, Customer Phone #,
Customer Email)

Purchase-Cash Disbursement Table (<u>Purchase #</u>, <u>Check #</u>)

Step 5:   Implement relationships using foreign keys.

The last step is to link tables using foreign keys. In our table structure, we use a single underline to indicate a foreign key. If there are necessary tables with a one-to-one relationship (those that should not be collapsed into one table), it does not matter which table's primary key becomes the foreign key in the other table but do not post both primary keys as foreign keys.

However, the primary key of the table with a one-to-many relationship always becomes the foreign key in the (1,1) entity's table. That way, we can make sure that each attribute of a record is single-valued for both tables. For example, to link the **Artist Table** with the **Purchase Table**, we add Artist ID to the Purchase Table as a foreign key, since each purchase transaction involves only one artist. The revised table structure of the Purchase Table is as follows: **Purchase Table** (<u>Purchase #</u>, Purchase Date, Purchase Amount, <u>Artist ID</u>). After determining the proper foreign keys, other revised table structures are listed as follows:

Inventory Table (<u>Item #</u>, Inventory Description, Inventory Cost, <u>Purchase #</u>, <u>Sale #</u>)

Sale Table (<u>Sale #</u>, Sale Date, Sale Amount, Payment Type, <u>Customer ID</u>, <u>Account #</u>)

Cash Disbursement Table (<u>Check #</u>, Disbursement Date, Payment Amount,
<u>Artist ID</u>, <u>Account #</u>)

The revised REA diagram, with table structures, is presented in Figure 2-6.

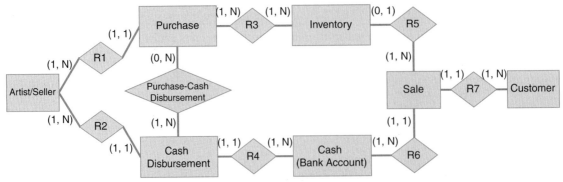

FIGURE 2-6   Cherokee's Revised REA Data Model

Inventory Table (Item #, Inventory Description, Inventory Cost, Purchase #, Sale #)

Cash Table (Account #, Account Type, Balance)

Sale Table (Sale #, Sale Date, Sale Amount, Payment Type, Customer ID, Account #)

Purchase Table (Purchase #, Purchase Date, Purchase Amount, Artist ID)

Cash Disbursement Table (Check #, Disbursement Date, Payment Amount, Artist ID, Account #)

Artist Table (Artist ID., Artist Name, Artist Address, Artist City, Artist State, Artist ZIP Code, Artist Phone #, Artist Email)

Customer Table (Customer ID, Customer Name, Customer Address, Customer City, Customer State, Customer ZIP Code, Customer Phone #, Customer Email)

Purchase-Cash Disbursement Table (Purchase #, Check #)

DATABASE ANOMALIES AND NORMALIZATION

Basic Concepts and Definitions

During logical data modeling, we often use general business knowledge and the understanding of the specific company to determine which attributes should be included in different tables. In general, after using the proper steps to create an REA data model (the logical design), the design of a database should not have serious flaws. However, before proceeding with physical design, we may want to validate the logical design. Normalization is a tool to validate and improve a logical design to satisfy database requirements and to avoid unnecessary duplication of data. It is the process of decomposing tables with anomalies to produce well-structured (often smaller) tables.

Three anomalies may occur when a table is not well designed. The **update anomaly** causes problems in updating a record. That is, updating a data value of one record needs to be done many times. Data inconsistency may occur due to this anomaly. The **insert anomaly** causes difficulty, sometimes impossibility, to insert new data into a table. The **delete anomaly** involves unintended loss of data that arises when deleting a row in a table. The following vendor table showing data from part of its entire table is used to explain these anomalies. The logical design of this original table presented in Figure 2-7 is: **Vendor Table 1** (Vendor#, Vendor Name, Vendor Address, Contact Name, Phone#, Item#, Description, Unit Price).

Since Vendor# is the primary key of this table, adding and deleting records should be based on Vendor#. This vendor table has update anomalies. For example, if we want to update the description of item K-8 from DVD player to Sony DVD, we have to search the entire table and change every occurrence of that description. Overlooking one row would create inconsistency in the database. This table also has insert anomalies. For example, if the company explored a few new models of the iPod and would like to enter the information into the database, it is not possible until the company finds a local vendor of the specific model. This is because the primary key of the table is Vendor#. According to the entity integrity rule,

Vendor#	Vendor Name	Vendor Address	Contact Name	Phone#	Item#	Description	Unit Price
2010	AXA, Inc.	22 Heaven Wood Drive	Annie White	234-3435	M-45	Blender	$15.99
					K-4	iPod	$65.00
2011	Sys Co.	2273 Morgan Street	John Doe	655-7512	D-12	LCD projector	$560.00
2021	MFS	46 Kings Square, #5	Rachelle Brown	234-7799	M-45	Blender	$18.00
					K-4	iPod	$63.80
2013	Lazard	8 Santa Ana	Ed King	734-0109	K-8	DVD player	$134.00
2014	XYZ Co.	19 Columbus	Lan Lee	878-1888	K-8	DVD player	$129.99

FIGURE 2-7 Partial Data in a Vendor Table

the primary key cannot be null. That is, without specific information of a vendor, we cannot insert any inventory data. The worst anomaly is the delete anomaly. If Sys Co. is out of business and we would like to delete its record from the database, we would accidentally delete the inventory information of LCD projectors if Sys Co. is the only one selling LCD projectors to the company.

Steps in Normalization

Normalization can be understood and accomplished in stages. Each stage corresponds to a normal form. In this book, we describe and illustrate the steps to reach first, second, and third normal forms. The fifth normal form is the highest level of normalization in which any remaining anomalies are removed.

Step 1: Remove any repeating groups (First Normal Form).
Any repeating groups must be separated into a different table to reach the first normal form. Repeating groups are those related attributes with multivalued data. In the above-mentioned vendor table, inventory information of item#, description, and unit price is a repeat group. These columns have multivalued data. Hence, to normalize the vendor table to first normal form, we need to make **Vendor Table 1** two tables: **Vendor Table 2** and **Inventory Table**. According to Figure 2-7, the attribute of Unit Price is vendor and item specific. Hence, we need to tentatively exclude this attribute from both tables so that they can reach the first normal form. After Step 1, the logical designs of the two tables are: **Vendor Table 2** (Vendor#, Vendor Name, Vendor Address, Contact Name, Phone#), and **Inventory Table** (Item#, Description).

Step 2: Remove any partial dependencies (Second Normal Form).
When we normalize a table, we need to make sure the decomposed tables are linked so data can be retrieved from them. Tentatively, let's use Item# with Vendor# in the vendor table as a concatenated key so we can add back the attribute of Unit Price to the new vendor table. This proposed table has a logic design as follows: **Vendor Table 3** (Vendor#, Item#, Vendor Name, Vendor Address, Contact Name, Phone#, Unit Price).

This proposed table has the problem of partial dependency. Partial dependency exists if any non-key attribute[7] is dependent on part, not all, of the primary key. That is,

---
[7]Non-key attributes are those attributes that are not the primary key.

Vendor Name, Vendor Address, Contact Name, Phone# are functionally dependent on Vendor# only, not both Vendor# and Item#. Only Unit Price is dependent on the whole primary key. Hence, we need to decompose **Vendor Table 3** into two tables: **Vendor Table 4** (Vendor#, Vendor Name, Vendor Address, Contact Name, Phone#), and Vendor-Inventory Table (Vendor#, Item#, Unit Price). The **Vendor-Inventory Table** is a relationship table to link the **Inventory Table** and **Vendor Table 4**. Examine Figure 2-7 again, we know that the relationship between the entities (i.e., vendor and inventory) is many-to-many. As we mentioned earlier, whenever there is a many-to-many relationship, we must use a relationship table to link the two entities. If we do not do so, the tables are not normalized.

Step 3:   Remove any transitive dependencies (Third Normal Form).

A transitive dependency in a table is a functional dependency between two or more non-key attributes. Refer to Figure 2-7, the attribute Description is dependent on Item#, not the primary key Vendor#, although Item# is dependent upon Vendor#. This is a case of transitive dependency. After our first two steps of normalization, we have also removed transitive dependency from the original table design. Our final results of normalization are three tables:

Inventory Table (Item#, Description)

Vendor Table 4 (Vendor#, Vendor Name, Vendor Address, Contact Name, Phone#)

Vendor-Inventory Table (Vendor#, Item#, Unit Price)

Summary of Normalization

Normalization is a formal process to determine which attributes should be grouped together in a table. It validates the logical design to avoid any violation of database requirements. Normalization is done by decomposing a table with anomalies into smaller, well-structured tables. A table is in first normal form (1NF) if it contains no repeating groups (multivalued attributes). A table is in second normal form (2NF) if it is in first normal form and if every non-key attribute is fully dependent on the primary key. A table is in third normal form (3NF) if it is in second normal form and if all the non-key attributes are independent from each other (i.e., no transitive dependency). Any table at third normal form will have no update anomaly, no insert anomaly, and no delete anomaly.

KEY TERMS

primary key	concatenated/composite key	insert anomaly
foreign key	relationship tables	delete anomaly
entity integrity rule	normalization	third normal form
referential integrity rule	update anomaly	

QUESTIONS AND PROBLEMS FOR REVIEW

MULTIPLE-CHOICE QUESTIONS

2.1 In designing a database, what is the referential integrity rule?

(a) The primary key in a table should not be null.

(b) The foreign key in a table should not be null.

  (c) Each table must have a primary key and a foreign key.

  (d) Two of the above are correct.

  (e) None of the above is correct.

2.2 In designing a database, what is the entity integrity rule?

  (a) The primary key in a table should not be null.

  (b) The foreign key in a table should not be null.

  (c) Each table must have a primary key and a foreign key.

  (d) Two of the above are correct.

  (e) None of the above is correct.

2.3 Which table has repeating groups?

  (a) **Student Table** (Student ID, Student Name, Major, GPA)

  (b) **Student Table** (Student ID, Student Name, Major, Course#, Course Title)

  (c) **Student Table** (Student ID, Student Name, Major, Faculty Advisor)

  (d) Two of the above have repeating groups.

  (e) None of the above have repeating groups.

2.4 Which table has transitive dependency?

  (a) **Student Table** (Student ID, Student Name, Major, Courses Taken, Grade)

  (b) **Student Table** (Student ID, Student Name, Major, Course#, Course Title, Grade)

  (c) **Student Table** (Student ID, Student Name, Major, Faculty Advisor, Faculty Office#)

  (d) Two of the above have transitive dependency.

  (e) None of the above have transitive dependency.

2.5 How many tables are necessary to build a database according to the following data model?

  (a) 6

  (b) 7

  (c) 8

  (d) 9

  (e) 10

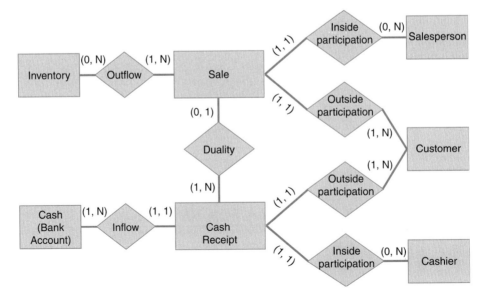

PROBLEMS

2.1 **Creating an REA Diagram based on given tables**

Examine the following tables and indicate the primary key (using PK) and the foreign key(s) (using FK) for each table. Based on the given tables, draw a **complete** REA diagram for the database.

Inventory				
Item_No	Description	Unit Cost	Unit Price	QOH
2010	Blender	14.00	29.95	100
2015	Toaster	12.00	19.95	200
2020	Mixer	23.00	33.95	150
2025	Television	499.00	699.95	95
2030	Freezer	799.00	999.95	52
2035	Refrigerator	699.00	849.95	75
2040	Radio	45.00	79.95	200
2045	Clock	79.00	99.95	150

Salesperson	
Salesperson_No	Salesperson_Name
101	John Smith
102	Brenda Kim
103	Julia Berens
104	Joe McGuire

Cashier	
Cashier_No	Name
201	Scott Brown
202	Stony Lee
203	Jim White
204	Pat Thomas

Customer				
Customer_No	Name	City	State	Credit _Limit
1000	Smith	Phoenix	AZ	2500
1001	Jones	St. Louis	MO	1500
1002	Jeffries	Atlanta	GA	4000
1003	Gilkey	Phoenix	AZ	5000
1004	Lankford	Phoenix	AZ	2000
1005	Zeile	Chicago	IL	2000
1006	Pagnozzi	Salt Lake	UT	3000
1007	Arocha	Chicago	IL	1000

Sales				
Invoice_No	Date	Salesperson_No	Customer_No	Amount
101	4/03/2006	101	1000	1549.90
102	4/05/2006	103	1003	299.85
103	4/05/2006	103	1002	1449.80
104	4/15/2006	104	1000	799.90
105	4/15/2006	102	1005	849.95
106	4/16/2006	102	1007	99.95
107	5/02/2006	101	1002	2209.70
108	5/03/2006	103	1000	799.90

Sales-Inventory			
Invoice_No	Item_No	Quantity	Extension
101	1025	1	699.95
101	1035	1	849.95
102	1045	3	299.85
103	1010	1	29.95
103	1015	1	19.95
103	1025	2	1399.95
104	1025	1	699.95
104	1045	1	99.95
105	1035	1	849.95
106	1045	1	99.95
107	1030	1	999.95
107	1035	1	849.95
107	1040	2	159.90
107	1045	2	199.90
108	1025	1	699.95
108	1045	1	99.95

Cash Collections					
Rimittance_No	Date	Amount	Invoice_No	Cashier_No	Customer_No
220	5/02/2006	1549.90	101	203	1000
278	5/10/2006	799.90	108	202	1000
276	5/30/2006	2209.70	107	202	1002
289	5/30/2006	849.95	105	204	1005

2.2 Cardinalities

Considering each business situation, indicate the maximum and minimum cardinalities for the following events. The first one is done for you.

Business situations	Cardinalities	
	Sales	**Cash collections**
1. Cash sales	(1,1)	(1,1)
2. Installment sales for firms like car dealers; down payment is required.		
3. The company often has credit sales. Customers must pay full amount for each transaction.		
	Sales	**Inventory**
4. A regular retail store that sells low-cost, mass-produced items and often carries new items.		
5. A construction company that builds custom homes only.		

2.3 Normalize a wholesale company's database

Given below is the design of a Sales table for a wholesale company. Indicate the primary key for the table. Given the current design of this table, list two violations of the basic requirements of a relational data model. Indicate possible anomalies in the table and then normalize the table to third normal form.

SO#	Invoice Date	Item #	Description	Quantity Ordered	Unit Price	Customer#	Customer Name
101	7/5/2006	2033	Washer	5	$359.99	22	Brown Co.
		2051	Dryer	8	$372.00		
102	7/5/2006	1099	TV	4	$258.00	26	Homebase
103	7/6/2006	2028	VCR	10	$179.99	24	Easy Shop
		2034	CD player	10	$185.00		
		2045	DVD player	5	$200.00		
104	7/8/2000	1099	TV	15	$258.00	22	Brown Co.

2.4 Normalize a library's database

Given below is the table of data for a library. First, determine which attribute is the best primary key. Second, examine the table and indicate the anomalies that may occur with the original design of this database. Why? Third, normalize the table into the third normal form to prepare it for use in a relational database environment.

Call#	Title	Borrower ID#	First Name	Last Name	Date Out	Date Due
K561.02	Soccer	S551442	John	Austin	12-03-05	01-03-06
D221.67	US Presidents	S702361	James	Wilson	12-20-05	01-20-06
I264.89	HR Laws & Regulations	F012618	Mark	Ding	12-20-05	03-20-06
H122.34	Volcanoes	S702361	James	Wilson	12-20-05	01-20-06
K249.02	Swimming	S002579	Freddie	Sunder	01-03-06	02-03-06
M426.52	Egypt	S002579	Freddie	Sunder	01-03-06	02-03-06
K922.4	Badminton	F012618	Mark	Ding	01-05-06	04-05-06

2.5   Quest, Inc.

The following tables and attributes exist in a relational database of Quest, Inc. First, draw a complete REA diagram for this database. **You must include cardinalities**. Determine the proper cardinalities based on the given design of each table and the additional information. Next, indicate if any errors exist in the given database design.

Table	Attributes
Vendor	Vendor#, Name, Address, City, State, Contact person, Phone, Fax
Purchases	P.O.#, Order date, Amount, Vendor#, Employee#
Employee	Employee#, Name, Address, Home phone number, Date hired
Purchase-Inventory	P.O.#, Item#, Unit cost, Quantity purchased, Extension
Purchase-Cash Disbursement	P.O.#, Disbursement voucher#
Inventory	Item#, Description, Quantity on hand
Cash	Bank account#, Bank name, Bank address, Balance
Cash Disbursement	Disbursement voucher#, Check#, Date, Amount

Additional information:

- Quest is a retail company and it often carries new items of inventories.
- Quest would like to include potential vendors in its vendor table.
- Most vendors allow credit purchases.
- Use the same employee table for internal agents.

CHAPTER 3

USING ACCESS *TO IMPLEMENT* A RELATIONAL DATABASE

INTRODUCTION

This chapter introduces the *Microsoft Access* database management system (DBMS) to provide hands-on practice in designing a database. After completing this chapter, you should be able to:

- Understand the *Access* objects, including tables, queries, forms, reports, pages, and macros
- Create, open, and display tables based on the data model
- Create forms to enter data into tables
- Establish relationships among tables

MICROSOFT ACCESS

Most integrated information systems use databases. The software program that defines the database; provides for simplified data entry; manipulates, stores, and retrieves data; and produces reports from the data is called the *database management system* (DBMS). *Microsoft Access* (*Access*) is a relational DBMS. *Access* refers to the structures and methods used to manage the data as objects. There are seven types of objects as seen in the left column of the *Access* database window in Figure 3-1.

Tables are the most important object. As you have already learned, a relational database means that the data is stored in tables or relations. Similar to a file, a table is considered as a file to store/collect data. Thus, the various tables contain *all* the data in a relational database.

Queries allow the user to ask questions about the data stored in the database. For example, queries can be used to locate and display a subset of the records of a table (called a "dynaset"), to modify data by combining information from several tables into a single result, to perform calculations on fields, or to specify criteria for searching the data.

Forms allow the user to see data from tables in another view, usually one record at a time. This often facilitates data entry. Forms can be customized so that they are an exact copy of an existing paper form, making it easier to move from hard copy to soft copy. In a fully automated setting, the form could be filled out on screen at the time of purchase removing a step and greatly enhancing the simplicity and accuracy of data entry.

Reports utilize data created from queries and/or from one or more tables to provide the user with meaningful information in a printed format. Data can be sorted, grouped, and summarized in almost limitless arrangements in reports. As a result, using reports, you can

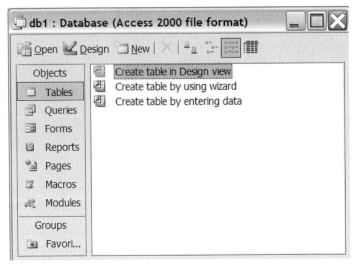

FIGURE 3-1

produce documents such as invoices, purchase orders, sales summaries, and financial statements. However, whereas you can enter and edit the data in a Form, you cannot do so with the data in a Report.

Pages (or data access pages) create a Web-based form with the benefit of being able to handle live data from the Internet or an intranet outside of the *Access* database.

Macros are an advanced *Access* object. A macro performs specific, user-specified, automated tasks, such as opening a form, printing a report, or going to the last record. Macros can also assist in the creation of turnkey applications that anyone can use, whether or not they have experience with *Access*.

Modules are an even more advanced *Access* object than Macros. Using Modules, you can create and edit Visual Basic code or procedures for the database. Modules are the containers used to organize the code.

Creating and Opening a Database

To create a new database in *Access*, you must first launch the *Access* application. When you launch Access, you will notice a **Getting Started** dialog box on the right hand side of the screen. At the bottom of this dialog box, you will see a selection enabling you to **Create A New File** (see Figure 3-2).

Click **Create A New File** and a new screen pops up (Figure 3-3). This function is also available under the **File** menu and under the **New** ☐ icon.

Now click on **Blank Database** under **New**. You should now see the **File New Database** window, as shown in Figure 3-4. A default name of *db1.mdb* will appear in the **File name text box** at the bottom of the window. Type over this name and create a database named **Cherokee**. Note that typing the extension *.mdb* is optional because *Access* automatically supplies it if you do not.

Click the **Create** button. Access will automatically open your new database for you (Figure 3-5).

FIGURE 3-2

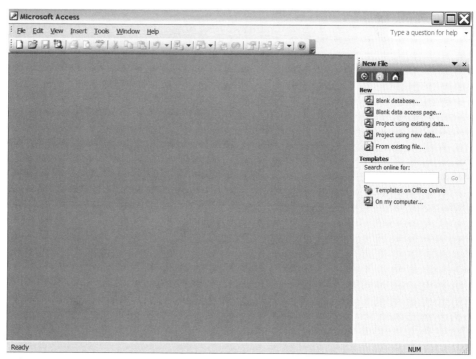

FIGURE 3-3

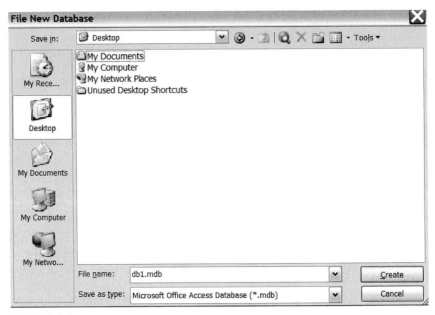

FIGURE 3-4

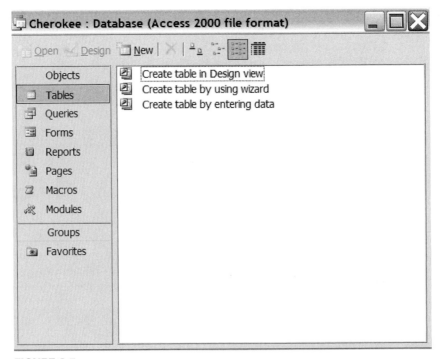

FIGURE 3-5

Creating and Opening a Table

You will notice in Figure 3-5 that there are three ways to create a new table: (1) Create a table in Design view; (2) Create a table using wizard (i.e., to select a prebuilt table that is complete with generic field definitions); and (3) Create a table by entering data (entering data into a spreadsheet view). Since Cherokee's tables have been designed as a result of creating the REA diagram and we do not have any data for the tables yet, we should create a table in design view.

1. To create a table, be sure you have selected the **Tables** tab in the Database window. Click on the **Design** icon or click on **Create table in Design view** (Figure 3-5). A Table window is displayed which contains three columns: **Field Name, Data Type, and Description** as shown in Figure 3-6.

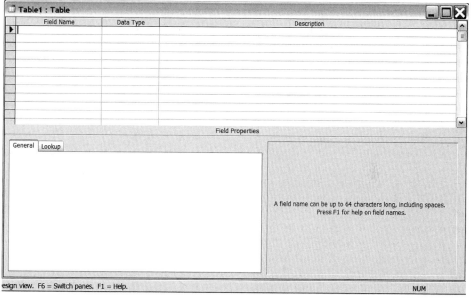

FIGURE 3-6

Field Names can be up to 64 characters and can include any combination of letters, numbers, spaces, and special characters (**except** a period, an exclamation point, a backquote character, or brackets because they are reserved *Microsoft Visual Basic* operators). In addition, obviously a **Field Name** cannot contain leading spaces.

Although a Field Name can include spaces, spaces in names could produce naming conflicts in Microsoft Visual Basic *in some circumstances. Therefore, we will adopt a convention of omitting the spaces in our Field Names and simply capitalizing each new word in the Field Name.*

When you tab to the **Data Type** column, you will note a button to pull down a menu. This button allows you to select the **Data Type** for the given **Field Name**. Take some time to explore the various **Data Types**. The **Description** property is used to provide useful information about the table or query and its fields.

2. Create the **Customer Table** for Cherokee.

In Chapter 2, based on the REA diagram, we created the conceptual model of a database for Cherokee. The table structures are as follows:

Inventory Table (<u>Item #</u>, Inventory Description, Inventory Cost, <u><u>Purchase #</u></u>, <u><u>Sale #</u></u>)

Cash Table (<u>Account #</u>, Account Type, Balance)

Sale Table (<u>Sale #</u>, Sale Date, Sale Amount, Payment Type, <u>Customer ID</u>, <u>Account #</u>)

Purchase Table (<u>Purchase #</u>, Purchase Date, Purchase Amount, <u>Artist ID</u>)

Cash Disbursement Table (<u>Check #</u>, Disbursement Date, Payment Amount,

Artist ID, <u>Account #</u>)

Artist Table   (<u>Artist ID</u>, Artist Name, Artist Address, Artist City, Artist State, Artist ZIP Code, Artist Phone #, Artist Email)

Customer Table   (<u>Customer ID</u>, Customer Name, Customer Address, Customer City, Customer State, Customer ZIP Code, Customer Phone #, Customer Email)

Purchase-Cash Disbursement Table (<u>Purchase #</u>, <u>Check #</u>)

Check the table structure of the **Customer Table**. It has the following attributes: ID, Name, Address, City, State, ZIP Code, phone #, and Email. Type **CustomerID** as the first attribute in the Field Name column. When creating a table, it is very important that you check your work. Before you tab out of the Field Name, make it a habit to check your spelling. Field Names are created when you establish table structures. Everything you do in a database is written in the data dictionary. Therefore, a database can increase in size very quickly. On the practical side, this can create storage problems. However, let's assume that this isn't a problem and you create a Field Name that you later realize you want to change. You can then go back and change it but you may want to make sure that it is identical to every other instance in which it appears (i.e., every other table in which you may have used it as a foreign key).

3. Once you have checked your field name, press enter or the Tab key. Make **CustomerID** the primary key by clicking the **Primary Key** 🔑 toolbar button.

As we discussed earlier, a primary key is an attribute that uniquely identifies each record. By defining a primary key, Access *does three things:*

- It automatically insures that no two records in that table will have the same value in the primary key field.
- It keeps records sorted according to the primary key field.
- It speeds up processing.

4. We will set its data type to **Text** assuming that Cherokee uses a combination of letters and numbers to identify their customers. A data type of **Text** can store data consisting of either text or number characters. If you hit the **Save** 💾 button, you will get a pop up window asking for the table name. Type in **Customer Table**.

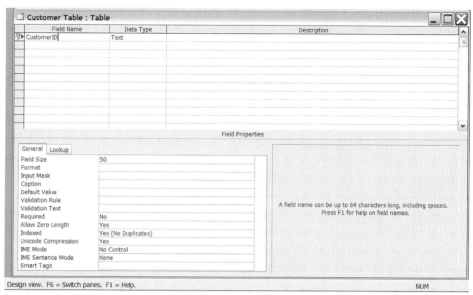

FIGURE 3-7

Notice that when you move from the **Field Name** column to the **Data Type** column, a **Field Properties** pane is displayed at the bottom of the screen. As noted at the bottom of the screen in Figure 3-7, you can toggle to the **Field Properties** pane by pressing **F6** or you can move to the **Field Properties** pane by moving your mouse to the desired field. This pane allows the user to specify the properties for the chosen field and type.

Data Input Controls

Data input controls deal with the accuracy and completeness of data that are entered into the database. Some of the most important input controls are data entry verification such as closed-loop verification, completeness control, (discussed later) and edit checks. Edit checks are incorporated into the design of each field to verify and validate the accuracy of data. Table 3-1 describes the most important field properties in *Access*. Most of these can be used as edit checks.

5. Press **F6** to switch to the Field Properties pane of the Table window and set the properties as described in Table 3-2.

6. The Data Types for all subsequent fields in the **Customer Table** should be set to **Text**. The second Field Name should be **CustomerName**, the Field Size is **45**, and the Caption should be **Customer Name**. The third Field Name should be **CustomerAddress**, the Field Size is **35**, and the Caption should be **Address**. The fourth Field Name should be **CustomerCity**, the field size is **25**, and the Caption should be **City**. The fifth Field Name should be **CustomerState**. The Field Size is **2**. In the Field Properties pane, set the Input Mask property for the **CustomerState** field by typing >**LL** as shown in Figure 3-8. The ">" symbol means that everything that follows will be in uppercase. An "L" symbol means that it must be a letter. Therefore, this input mask will result in any input being changed to two capital letters. For example, if you were to type "ca," *Access* would change the input

Table 3-1 Field Properties in Access

Field Property	Description
Field Size	Sets the maximum size for data stored in a Text, Number, or AutoNumber field. In a Text field, the default size is 50, but the size may range from 1 to 255. In Number fields, the default is set to Long Integer.
Format	Specifies how data are to be displayed in a field. Particularly useful in specifying the format for numbers, currency, dates, and times.
Decimal Places	Specifies the number of digits allowed to the right of the decimal point. Auto allows the Format property to determine the number of decimal places automatically.
Input Mask	Makes data entry easier by adjusting the data entered so that it conforms to the standard set in the Input Mask. Also used to control the values users can enter. Review the InputMask property help screen to familiarize yourself with this property. See Steps 6–8 below.
Caption	Specifies the text for labels attached to controls created by dragging a field from the field list, and serves as the column heading for the field when the table or query is in Datasheet view. Captions should be descriptive of the Field Names they relate to since they will be used as headings for the data in creating Forms and Reports.
Default Value	Specifies a default value for a field (e.g., San Jose can be set as the Default Value for a City field; the user then has the option of accepting the Default Value or inputting different data).
Validation Rule	Specifies the requirements and limits the values allowed for data entry. For example, the Validation Rule may begin with the word "Like" and continue on with a series of characters placed in quotes to set the requirements for data to be entered into the field. The meaning of these characters is found under the Input Mask Syntax and Examples help screen. Review the Validation Rule property help screen to familiarize yourself with this property.
Validation Text	The text input in the Validation Text property specifies the message to be displayed to the user when the Validation Rule is violated. For example, when a record is added for a new employee, you can require that the entry in the Start Date field fall between the company's founding date and the current date. If the date entered isn't in this range, you can display the message: "Start date is incorrect."
Required	Specifies whether or not a value is required in a field; if Yes, the field requires a value, if No, no entry is required.
Allow Zero Length	Indicates whether an empty string (i.e., a string containing no characters) is a valid entry; if Yes, the field will accept an empty string even when the Required property is set to Yes.
Indexed	This sets a single-field index (i.e., a feature that speeds the sorting and searching of a table by allowing the program to do a speed search on the field). The primary key is always indexed. When a field is indexed, it is also necessary to specify whether duplicates will be allowed. For example, when creating a purchase table, the primary key might be Purchase# and you would not want to allow duplicates. However, when creating a table to add the inventory purchased on a particular purchase, you might still want to be able to sort and search based upon the Purchase# (which would require that field to be indexed), but you would expect that a particular purchase might have several items of inventory. Therefore, duplicates would be allowed.

Table 3-2

Field Size	6
Caption	Customer ID
Validation Rule	Like "???###" (see Table 3-1)
Validation Text	Incorrect Customer ID format. The Customer ID must consist of three letters and three numbers.
Required	Yes
Indexed	No duplicates

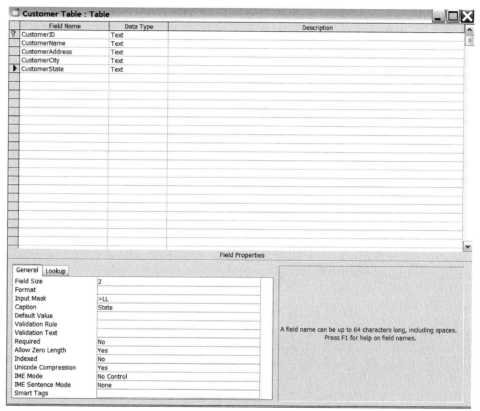

FIGURE 3-8

to "CA" so that it conformed to the standard input required by the input mask. Use an appropriate Caption for the **CustomerState** field.

7. The sixth Field Name should be **CustomerZIPCode**. The Field Size is **10**. Activate the **Input Mask Wizard** (the button with three small dots located in the Input Mask Property; see Figure 3-9) to aid in making a template for the Zip Code. You will be prompted to save the table first. Click Yes.

Select Zip Code from the menu (see Figure 3-10), click **Next** twice, and choose the Zip Code with the hyphen. Click on **Finish**.

Use an appropriate Caption for this field.

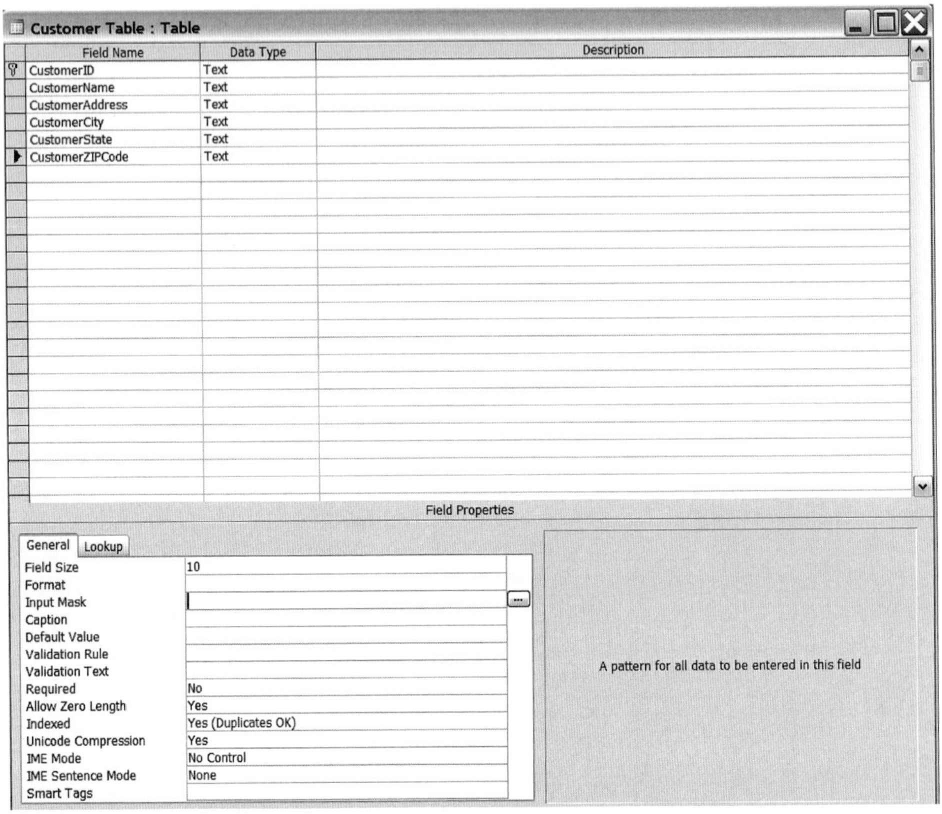

Field Name	Data Type	Description
CustomerID	Text	
CustomerName	Text	
CustomerAddress	Text	
CustomerCity	Text	
CustomerState	Text	
CustomerZIPCode	Text	

Field Properties

General | Lookup

Field Size	10
Format	
Input Mask	
Caption	
Default Value	
Validation Rule	
Validation Text	
Required	No
Allow Zero Length	Yes
Indexed	Yes (Duplicates OK)
Unicode Compression	Yes
IME Mode	No Control
IME Sentence Mode	None
Smart Tags	

A pattern for all data to be entered in this field

FIGURE 3-9

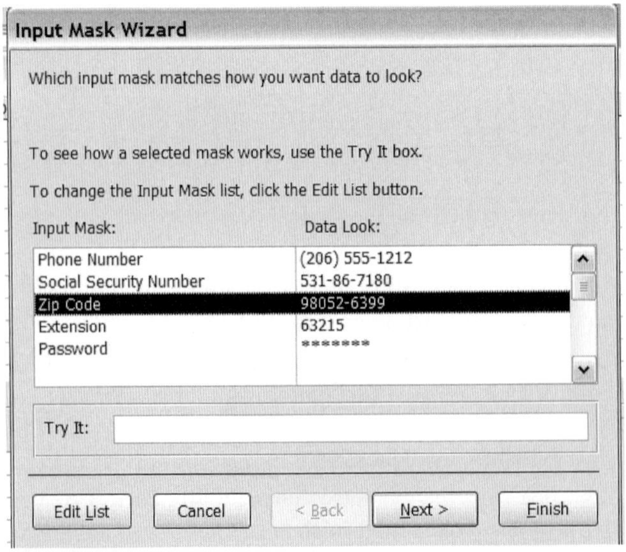

Input Mask Wizard

Which input mask matches how you want data to look?

To see how a selected mask works, use the Try It box.

To change the Input Mask list, click the Edit List button.

Input Mask:	Data Look:
Phone Number	(206) 555-1212
Social Security Number	531-86-7180
Zip Code	98052-6399
Extension	63215
Password	*******

Try It:

Edit List | Cancel | < Back | Next > | Finish

FIGURE 3-10

Table 3-3

Field Size	6
Caption	Artist ID
Validation Rule	Like "???###"
Validation Text	Incorrect Artist ID format. The Artist ID must consist of three letters and three numbers.
Required	No
Indexed	No duplicates

8. The seventh Field Name is **CustomerPhone#**. The Field Size is **14**. The Caption is Customer Telephone Number. Use the Input Mask Wizard to set the Input Mask property to the predefined Phone Number setting.

9. The last field is called **CustomerEmail**. The Field Size is **35**; use an appropriate Caption.

10. Congratulations! You are now finished with the table. When you close this object and all objects in the future, use the "X" in the upper right hand corner of the screen to save and close the object.

Now we will create the **Artist Table**.

1. Create a new table in Design view as you did before.

2. Create the **Artist Table** in a similar way as you did for the **Customer Table**. The **ArtistID** will be the Primary Key. Its properties should be as described in Table 3-3.

3. Refer to Cherokee's **Customer Table** structure for the remaining fields in the **Artist Table**. Use field sizes similar to those used in the **Customer Table**.

Completeness Control

Completeness is an important component in internal control. Completeness suggests not only that all data in a transaction are captured, but also that all transactions are recorded. Therefore, it is important to ensure that no documents are lost or misplaced. One way to accomplish this is to prenumber documents and to verify the sequential integrity of the completed documents. We will use this feature in creating the **Purchase Table**.

1. Create a new table in Design view.

2. Refer to Cherokee's table structure for the **Purchase Table**. The first attribute is **Purchase#**. This is the first Field Name. Choose **AutoNumber** as the Data Type. The Caption is **Purchase #**. Make this field the primary key by clicking the **Primary Key** toolbar button.

3. The second Field Name is **PurchaseDate**. The Data type is **Date/Time**. Use the Input Mask Wizard to create the Input Mask property. When prompted to save the table, save it as Purchase Table. Choose **Short Date** for the Input Mask as shown in Figure 3-11.

Click on **Next** twice and then click on **Finish**. After you tab out of the Input Mask property, it should look like this: **99/99/00;0;_**. The Caption is **Purchase Date**.

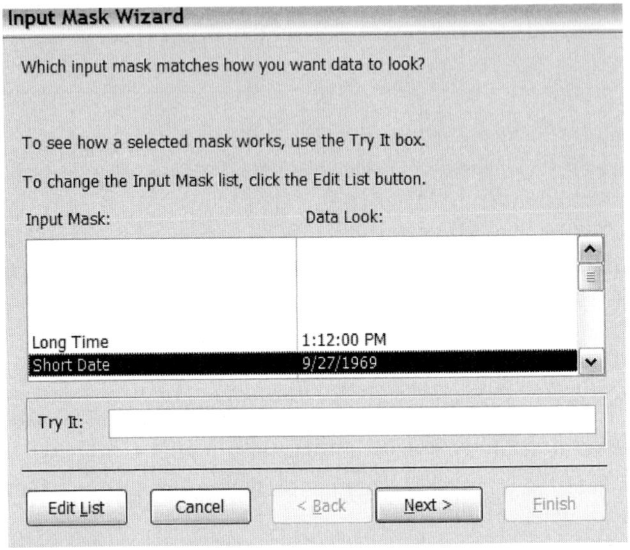

FIGURE 3-11

4. The third Field Name is **PurchaseAmount**. The Data Type is **Currency**. The Caption is **Purchase Amount**.

5. The fourth Field Name is **ArtistID**. The Data Type is **Text**. The field size is 6. The Caption is Artist ID.

*Notice that you have already used the Field Name **ArtistID**. It is the primary key in the **Artist Table**. As we mentioned before, when a field name appears in one table that is a primary key in another table, it is called a **Foreign Key**. Foreign keys are used to link tables together. A foreign key must be the same data type as the corresponding primary key it will be linked to.*

6. You will now save the table as **Purchase Table**.

Creating and Opening a Form

Although the data can be entered from the datasheet view of a table, the utilization of forms makes data easier to enter and makes the database much more user-friendly. A form can display data in almost any format. A very simple form can be designed to display one record at a time. More complex forms can be created as 'fill-in-the-blanks' forms resembling the paper forms a company already uses.

1. Before entering data into the **Customer Table**, you will create a form utilizing the **Form Wizard** as indicated in Figure 3-12. Double click the selection of Create form by using wizard.

2. In the form wizard window (see Figure 3-13), use the pull down menu to choose **Customer Table** and select for inclusion in the form all fields created in the table by clicking on the ≫ button in the middle of the window. Then click on **Next**.

3. The wizard's next window allows you to choose a layout. Take some time to view each of the various layouts and then select the **Columnar** format. Click **Next**.

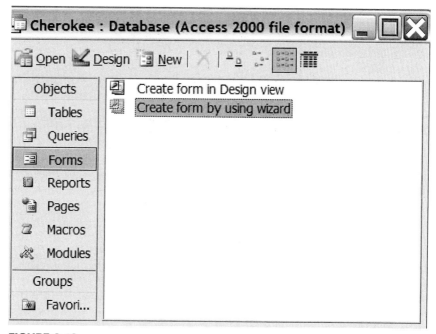

FIGURE 3-12

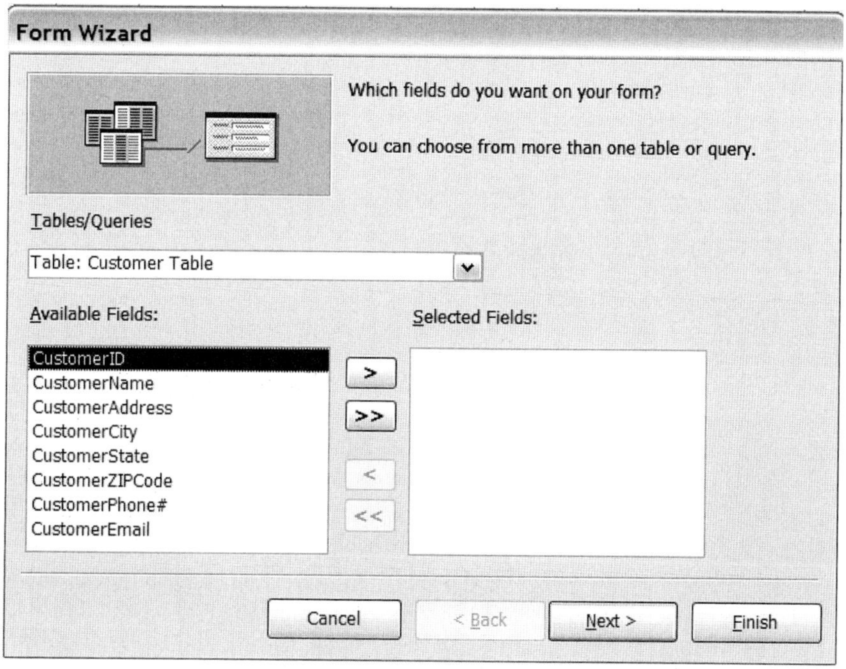

FIGURE 3-13

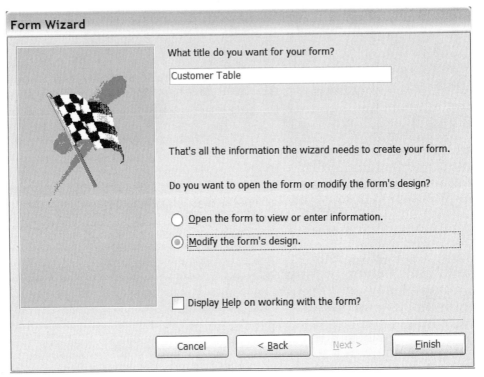

FIGURE 3-14

4. You are now presented with a selection of styles or backgrounds from which to choose (not illustrated). Again take some time to view each of the styles. Keep your users in mind when you choose a style and pick one that will be user-friendly. Click **Next** again.

5. Type **Customer Form** for the title. Select **Modify the form's design** as indicated in Figure 3-14. Click **Finish** and a screen resembling Figure 3-15 will appear.

6. To enlarge the form's work area, place the mouse on the right side of the work area (the dotted area) until the crosshairs appear. Click and drag the mouse to the right enlarging the work area approximately one to two inches. Similarly, add space for a form title by placing the mouse between the Form Header bar and the Detail bar until the crosshairs appear. You can refer to *Access'* help function for further information regarding the names of various form segments. Click and drag the Detail bar down approximately one-half inch as shown in Figure 3-15.

7. Click the Label 🅰 icon on the form design toolbox to create a stand-alone label and draw a rectangle in the header window. If you do not see the toolbox, click the Toolbox 🛠 icon to get it. Type the label "**Customer Form.**" Click outside the label once and then click the label once. Notice that the **Format** toolbar is enabled. Format the label using a **bold**, size **18 font** (see Figure 3-16). Save the form and close it. Your **Customer Form** is now listed in the database.

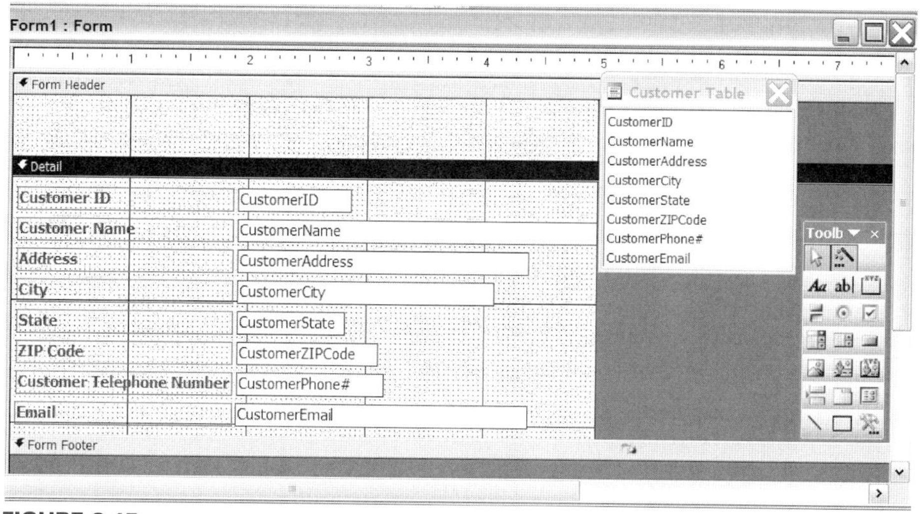

FIGURE 3-15

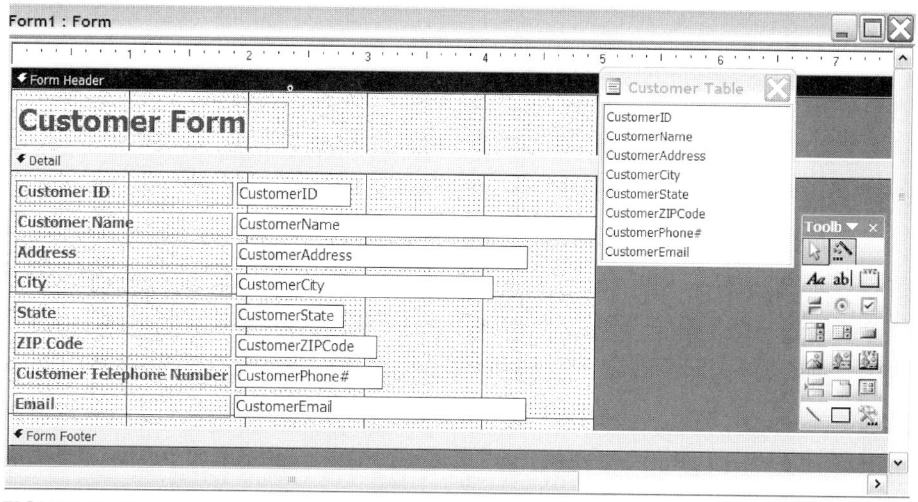

FIGURE 3-16

8. Open the Customer Form and now you see the form name changed from **Form1** to **Customer Form** (see Figure 3-17).

As you enter the information from the form view, pay attention to the size and caption of the fields. If need be, you can adjust the size by clicking on the **Design View** and stretching or shrinking the field and then toggling back to the form by clicking on the **Form View** icon in the Form Design toolbar at the top of the main screen. Since the caption for the customer's telephone number is too long, change it from **Customer**

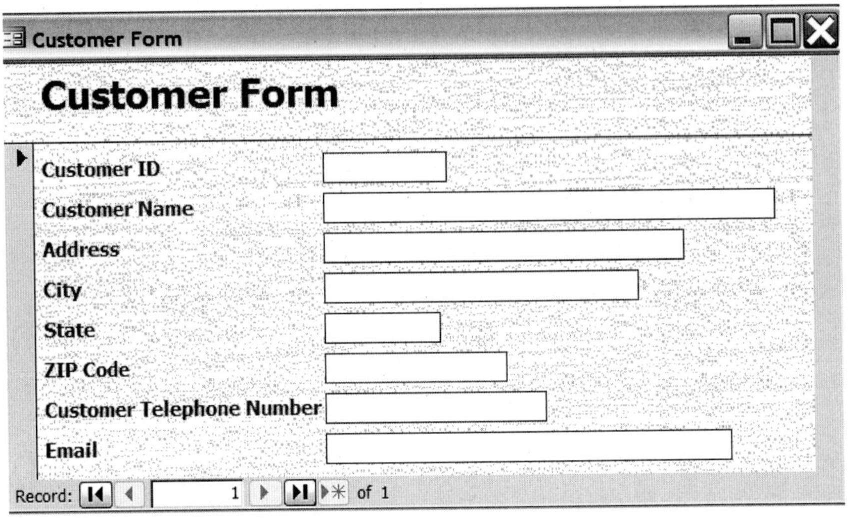

FIGURE 3-17

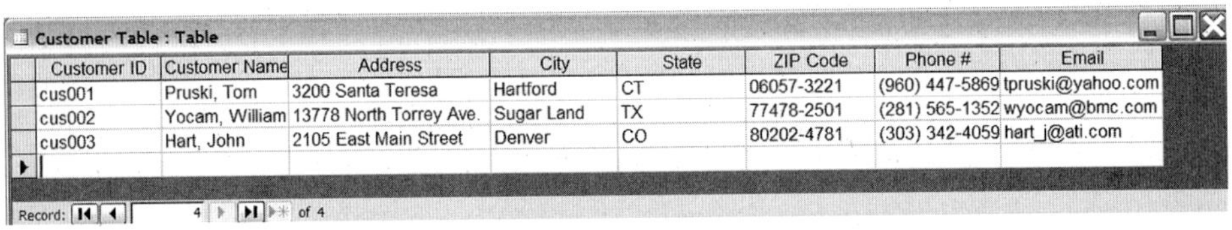

FIGURE 3-18

Telephone Number to **Phone #**. You need to make the adjustment in the **Design View** 📐. Enter customer information as shown in the datasheet view (Figure 3-18).

9. When you are finished adjusting the form's design and entering the data, close the form.

10. Using the same approach, create the Artist Form.

Creating Relationships to Link Tables

As stated previously, *Access* is a relational database. This implies that associations or relationships are created between attributes (columns) in two tables to link the data from one table to another. This is important because the relations allow the data to be brought together in forms and for reporting purposes. Thus, as a result of the relations we build into the database, we can very easily and quickly query the database to discover what customer purchased a particular piece of artwork. The REA model of Cherokee's expenditure cycle is reproduced in Figure 3-19 for review.

Since each artists' pieces can be purchased in any number of purchase events, there should be a one-to-many relationship established between the **Artist Table** and the **Purchase Table** so that data regarding artists does not have to be duplicated on the

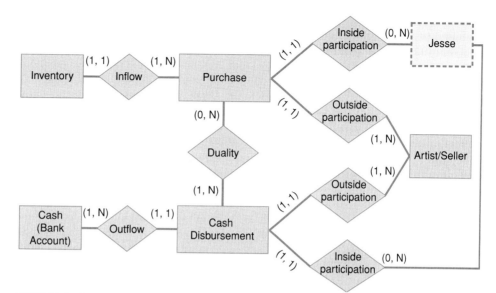

FIGURE 3-19 Complete REA Diagram for Cherokee's Expenditure Cycle

Purchase Table. Notice that in *Access*, only the maximum cardinality is shown in the relationship window.

In this section, you will set up these other tables for Cherokee and create relationships among them. The following instructions will aid in setting up a relationship linking the **Purchase Table** to the **Artist Table**.

1. From the main *Access* window, click on the Relationships ⚏ toolbar button (or select Relationships from the Tools menu).

2. In the Show Table window, add both the **Purchase Table** and the **Artist Table** as shown in Figure 3-20. Close the Show Table dialogue box.

Click and drag the **ArtistID** field in the **Artist Table** to the **ArtistID** field in the **Purchase Table**.

3. Click on the **Enforce Referential Integrity** checkbox as indicated in Figure 3-21. Referential integrity ensures that records referenced by a foreign key cannot be deleted unless the record containing the foreign key is first removed. Thus, in this case, an artist now cannot be deleted if there is a related purchase and you cannot delete an artist from the **Purchase Table** screen. In addition, enforcing referential integrity also checks to make sure that the two fields' data types match.

4. Click on the **Create** button (see Figure 3-22).

5. Save and close.

In this chapter, you learned how to construct tables and relationships in *Access* based on an REA diagram. Tables are the fundamental storage entity for the database. You also learned how to construct forms from the tables you created. Forms facilitate the entry and manipulation of the data. In the next chapters, we will explore queries and reports while we construct the Sales/Collection cycle, the Acquisition/Payment cycle, and the Human Resource cycle.

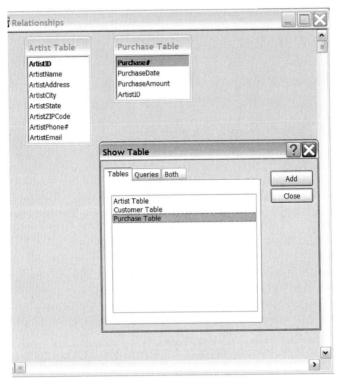

FIGURE 3-20

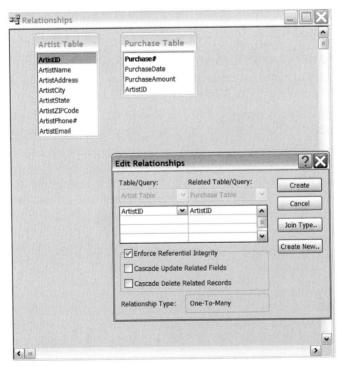

FIGURE 3-21

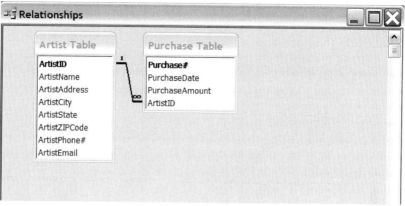

FIGURE 3-22

KEY TERMS

tables
queries
forms

reports
referential integrity
completeness control

validation rule
input mask

QUESTIONS AND PROBLEMS FOR REVIEW

MULTIPLE-CHOICE QUESTIONS

3.1 Which of the following are the objects in *Access*?
(a) Tables
(b) Forms
(c) Queries
(d) Reports
(e) All of the above.

3.2 In *Access*, we use tables in a database for
(a) Data entry
(b) Data storage
(c) Data retrieval
(d) Two of the above are correct.

3.3 In *Access*, we use forms in a database for
(a) Data entry
(b) Data storage
(c) Data retrieval
(d) Two of the above
(e) None of the above.

PROBLEMS

3.1 Cherokee Art and Antique Store—Tables and Relationships

You have created the Purchase Table, Artist Table, and Customer Table. Now, create the remaining tables and relationships for Cherokee using the established table structure.

Inventory Table (Item #, Inventory Description, Inventory Cost, Purchase #, Sale #)

Cash Table (Account #, Account Type, Balance)

Sale Table (Sale #, Sale Date, Sale Amount, Payment Type, Customer ID, Account #)

Purchase Table (Purchase #, Purchase Date, Purchase Amount, Artist ID)

Cash Disbursement Table (Check #, Disbursement Date, Payment Amount, Artist ID, Account #)

Artist Table (Artist ID, Artist Name, Artist Address, Artist City, Artist State, Artist ZIP Code, Artist Phone #, Artist Email)

Customer Table (Customer ID, Customer Name, Customer Address, Customer City, Customer State, Customer ZIP Code, Customer Phone #, Customer Email)

Purchase-Cash Disbursement Table (Purchase #, Check #)

3.2 Cherokee Art and Antique Store–Forms

Create a form for Cherokee to enter data into the Inventory Table.

CHAPTER 4

SALES/COLLECTION BUSINESS PROCESS

INTRODUCTION

In the previous chapter, we looked at a very simple revenue cycle for Cherokee Art and Antique Store. In this chapter, we will look at a more complex revenue cycle. In general, a *business process* is almost synonymous with a transaction cycle. The Sales/Collection business process is often referred to as the revenue transaction cycle. The Sales/Collection process includes the marketing events (i.e., sales calls, advertising campaigns, etc.), the mutual commitment events (i.e., customer orders), the economic decrement events (i.e., the sale and shipment), and the economic increment event (i.e., the cash receipt). We might also see an economic decrement reversal event (i.e., sales returns and allowances).

To model the Sales/Collection business process in a database, it will be useful to create more complex forms and we will begin to explore the creation of queries. After completing this chapter, you should be able to use *Microsoft Access* to:

- Create forms with subforms from tables for data entry.
- Create combo boxes in a form.
- Create queries involving single tables.
- Create queries involving simple calculations.
- Create queries involving more than one table.
- Create queries involving simple criteria.
- Create a simple report based on a query.

SALES/COLLECTION PROCESS OVERVIEW

Basic Concepts and Definitions

As you have learned in prior chapters, the revenue cycle interfaces with the conversion cycle, the financing cycle, and the financial reporting system. The financial reporting system then interfaces with the expenditure cycle and the payroll cycle.

By extending this concept to the framework of business processes, we can see that goods and services are made available to a company's Sales/Collection process as a result of the Conversion, Acquisition/Payment, and Payroll processes. The Sales/Collection process turns those goods and services into cash, which is made available to the Financing process. For this to happen, the Sales/Collection process must include at least one economic event that transfers out the goods and services (i.e., a decrement event). This is the sale event. It must also include at least one economic event that transfers in the cash (i.e., an increment event). This is the cash receipt event. The Sales/Collection process for all firms is similar regardless of whether the firm is engaged in manufacturing, in service, or in retail.

Labor is typically not tracked and matched to the revenue-generating activity since labor costs are normally aggregated into a selling, general, and administrative expense and tracked in the payroll cycle. One exception to this is in the case of service providers, where labor takes the place of inventory. Other exceptions include companies that use delivery services.

Tragg's Custom Surfboards

Background   Tragg's Custom Surfboards is located at 8713 Montauk Drive, La Selva Beach, CA 95076. Their telephone number is (831) 555-1513; their fax number is (831) 555-1613. Tragg's Custom Surfboards both manufactures and sells surfboards and surfing equipment. Dan Tragg began shaping, designing, and manufacturing his own surfboards 25 years ago. He soon discovered that there was a demand for them among his friends and acquaintances. He started selling them casually and ultimately founded the business in 1988. Initially, his boards were sold through a few select dealers. As demand grew however, he set up a Web site and opened his own store. The store now carries a stock of surfboards and Dan continues to fill custom orders.

Model the Revenue Cycle Using REA   As we did in Chapter 1 for Cherokee Art and Antique Store, we need to model the revenue cycle using the REA topology.[8] Since all sales are final, we will collapse the custom order event into the sales event for the sake of simplicity. Sales begin with the customer coming into the store or can commence through an e-mail or telephone call from the customer. Tragg's requires a 50 percent deposit before starting custom work and this deposit is nonrefundable. Custom orders usually take 4 to 5 weeks to complete.

Whether a custom order or a sale from existing stock, the customer has a choice between four basic board styles: Egotist, Imposer, Nice Devil, or King Creator. The customer can also choose between two fins: single fin or glassed-on fin. Coloring is offered in opaque or transparent. The customer can choose his or her own pigment for the board by sending in a color chip obtained from the paint section of their local hardware store.

Pricing is largely dependent upon the length of the board plus any extra features that are requested. For example, a board up to 6′11″ begins at $475. Anything longer than that goes up $25 in price for every 6 inches requested. All boards come with certain standard features, depending upon the board style chosen. In addition, the customer can add *only*

---

[8] Tragg's Custom Surfboards has more than just the economic increment and decrement events occurring. They have a marketing event (i.e., the Web site and the inquiries it generates). This is called the instigation event. In reality, there is also a mutual commitment event (i.e., the custom orders). For simplicity sake, however, we have chosen not to model these in this example.

one of the following custom extras: a pinline stripe for $20, a colored competition stripe for $40, color lamination (tint or opaque) for $40, cloth design for $50, airbrush finish for $25, gloss and polish for $45, or an extra 10-oz. Volan glass layer for $25. (Note that in reality customers would probably add more than one of these custom extras. We have limited it to one custom extra per order for simplicity's sake.) It is extremely rare that a customer does not customize his or her surfboard. Tragg's stores the information on extra features in a separate table.

When orders come in (custom orders or otherwise), a Sales Invoice form is completed. All sales are final; there are no returns allowed. As a result, the sales order is the sales invoice. (For simplicity of this example, we will assume that no sales tax is charged. In reality, sales tax would be charged on all in-store sales and Internet sales made to California residents.)

Customers must arrange to pick up the surfboards in the store or have them shipped. Final payment is due when the surfboard is picked up or before it is shipped. In addition, some customers may pay for several transactions at once (i.e., write one check for several invoices).

Although Tragg's maintains several bank accounts (one general checking account, one payroll account, and one savings account), most of the cash receipts and cash disbursements are handled through the general checking account. Most cash receipts come from sales. However, Tragg's does have a few investments that result in dividend income and are deposited in the general checking account.

According to the descriptions on Tragg's business processes in the revenue cycle, Figure 4-1 is an REA diagram created to model the business activities for Tragg's.

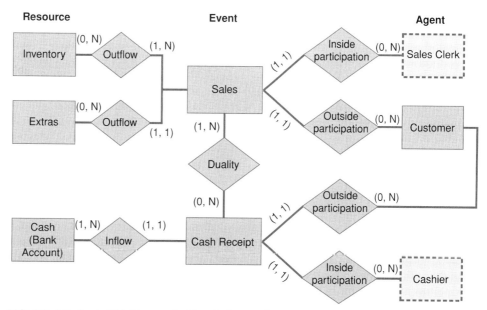

FIGURE 4-1 Basic REA Diagram for Tragg's Custom Surfboards Revenue Cycle

Create a Relational Database for Tragg's Following the REA Diagram

To start with a relatively simple design of a database, we will not create tables for those entities in dotted lines in Figure 4-1. In addition, as noted in the model, the relationship between entities Sales and Inventory is many-to-many. We do this because it is possible that we will have several of one particular kind, size, and color surfboard in stock at one time. These then can be further customized for customers in some way, if requested, or sold as is. Therefore, as you learned in Chapter 2, we cannot use a foreign key link to join these entities. You need a separate table to represent each many-to-many relationship.

Accordingly, Tragg's table structure for the Sales/Collection Business Process can be represented as follows:

Cash Table (CashAcctNo, AcctType)

Inventory Table (InventoryID, InventoryDescription, InventoryCost, InventoryPrice)

Extras Table (ExtrasID, ExtrasDescription, ExtrasCost, ExtrasPrice)

Cash Receipt Sale Table (CashReceiptID, InvoiceNo, AmountApplied)

Sales Inventory Table (InvoiceNo, InventoryID, QuantityOrdered, ExtrasID)

Cash Receipt Table (CashReceiptID, CRDate, CustomerCheckNo,

    CustomerID, CashAcctNo)

Sales Table (InvoiceNo, InvoiceDate, CustomerID)

Customer Table (CustomerID, CustomerLastName, CustomerFirstName,

    CustomerAddress1, CustomerAddress2, CustomerCity, CustomerState,
    CustomerZip, CustomerPhone)

Creating Tragg's Relational Database Using Access   Open the Chapter 4 database for Tragg's Custom Surfboards. Note that all the tables, some relationships, and some forms have already been created for the Sales/Collection business process. Take some time to examine the tables, forms, and the relationships that have been created thus far.

The Sales Form: Creating a Form with a Subform

Creating a **Sales Form** is a more complex task than creating the forms we have worked with in Chapter 3. After creating the **Sales Form**, we will be able to enter data into the **Sales Table** and the **Sales Inventory Table** at once. In addition, when we create the **Sales Form**, we will need data from the **Customer Table**, **Inventory Table**, and the **Extras Table**. Therefore, there must be data in these tables prior to creating a **Sales Form**. Open the Tragg's Custom Surfboard database and take some time to acquaint yourself with the **Customer Table**, **Inventory Table**, and the **Extras Table**. In addition, since creating the **Sales Form** is for entering data into the **Sales Table** and the **Sales Inventory Table**, we will need to establish the necessary relationships between all five tables before we create the form.

1. Click on the **Relationships** 🔲 icon to open the Relationships window.
2. Click on **Show Table** 🔲.

3. Hold down the **Ctrl** key and click on the **Customer Table**, the **Extras Table**, the **Inventory Table**, the **Sales Inventory Table**, and the **Sales Table**. Then click **Add** and click **Close**.

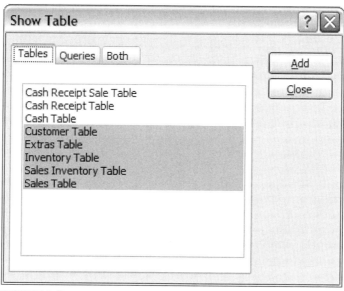

FIGURE 4-2

4. Create the necessary relationships by linking the primary keys to their foreign keys in the appropriate tables. For example, drag **CustomerID** from the **Customer Table** to **CustomerID** in the **Sales Table**. When you do this, the Edit Relationships window appears; click on the **Enforce Referential Integrity** button.

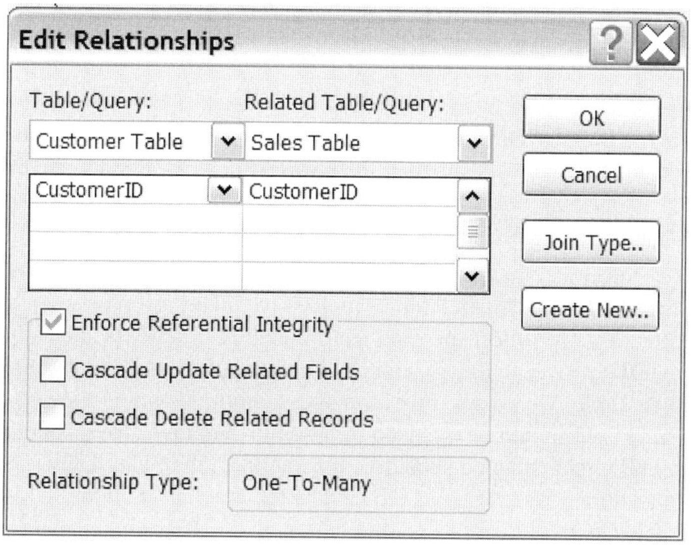

FIGURE 4-3

5. Create the other three necessary relationships.

6. Close the Relationships window.

Now that the Relationships have been created, we are ready to begin creating the **Sales Form**.

7. Click on the **Forms** object and double-click on **Create form by using wizard**.

8. From the Tables/Queries pull-down menu, select the **Sales Table** and select all three fields for inclusion in the form.

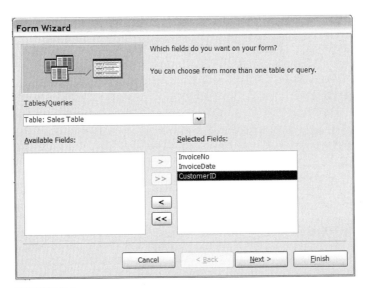

FIGURE 4-4

9. Select the **Customer Table** and select all the fields for inclusion in the form.

NOTE: Before you select fields for inclusion from this table and from tables in the future, it is important to be sure that the last field is highlighted in the Selected Fields window. If it is not, the fields may be out of order when the form is created and you might have to rearrange them!

10. Remember that in some cases a field represents a foreign key (i.e., it is a primary key in another table) and, therefore, provides the relationship between tables. Therefore, it is important that we select the field from the correct table for inclusion in the form. The **CustomerID** is one of these fields. It is represented in both the **Sales Table** and the **Customer Table**. We do not want to include both fields in the form so the question arises as to which field should be included in the **Sales Form**. Since this is the **Sales Form**, the **CustomerID** field included should be the one from the **Sales Table**.

In addition, there is no need to include the **CustomerPhone** field in the **Sales Form**. Return the **CustomerTable.CustomerID** and the **CustomerPhone** fields back to the Available Fields window.

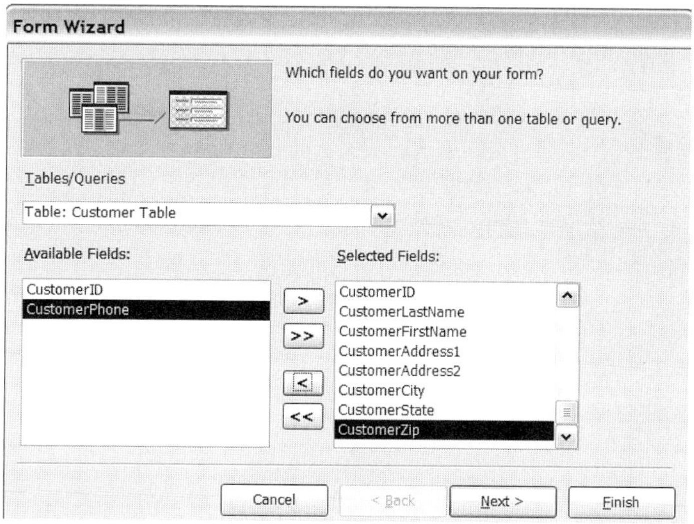

FIGURE 4-5

11. Select the **Sales Inventory Table** and, as before, select all fields for inclusion. Return the **Sales Inventory Table.InvoiceNo** field to the Available Fields window. We have already included the **InvoiceNo** field from the **Sales Table**. Therefore, we do not include it again from the **Sales Inventory Table**.

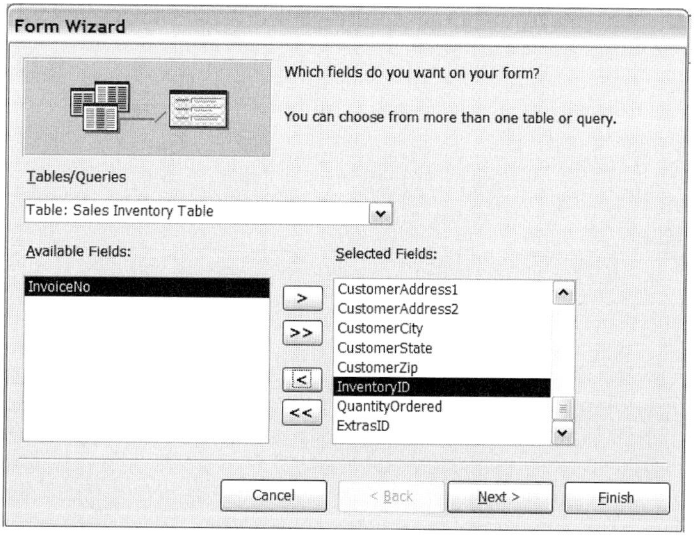

FIGURE 4-6

12. Select **Inventory Table** and select **InventoryDescription** and **InventoryPrice** for inclusion in the form. Note that you do not need the **InventoryTable.InventoryID**

field included in the form because you have already included this field when you added it from the **Sales Inventory Table**.

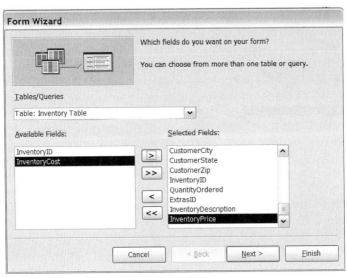

FIGURE 4-7

13. Select the **Extras Table** and select **ExtrasDescription** and **ExtrasPrice** for inclusion in the form. Note again that, just as you did not need to include the **Inventory Table.InventoryID** field, you do not need to include the **ExtrasID** from the **Extras Table** because you have already included this field when you added it from the **Sales Inventory Table**.

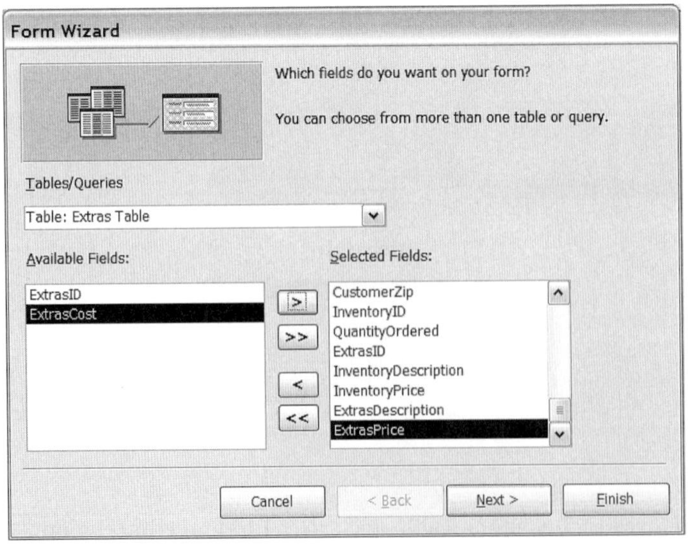

FIGURE 4-8

14. Click the **Next** button. The Form Wizard automatically suggests a layout for the **Sales Form** (containing fields from the **Sales Table** and the **Customer Table**) with a sub-form (containing the fields from the **Sales Inventory Table**, the **Inventory Table**, and the **Extras Table**).

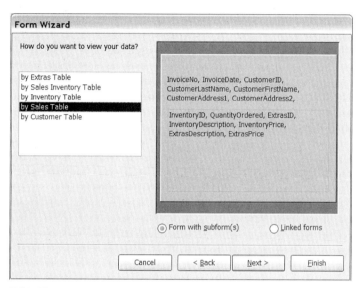

FIGURE 4-9

Accept the layout by clicking the **Next** button.

15. Select the Tabular layout for the subform in the next window and click **Next**. Select a style for your form and click **Next**. (Note that we have chosen to use Sumi Painting in all of our Forms.) Change the name of the form to **Sales Form** (leave the name of the subform alone). Click on **Modify the form's design**. Click on **Finish**.

16. Stretch the form out to 8½ inches.

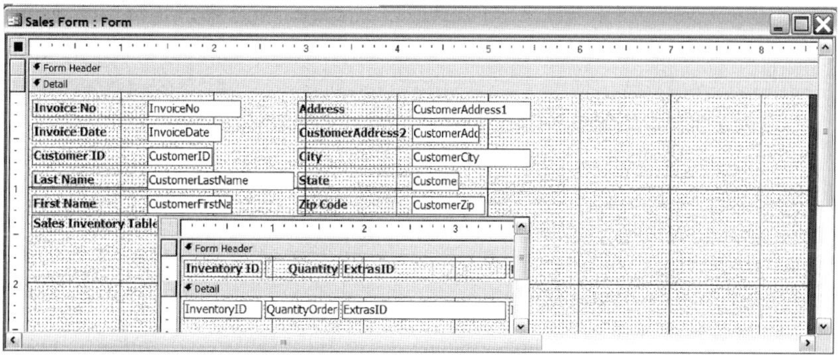

FIGURE 4-10

17. Switch to the Form View by clicking on the **View** ⊞ icon. Notice that the customer information is spread out in two columns and the city, state, and zip code portions of the address are on separate lines.

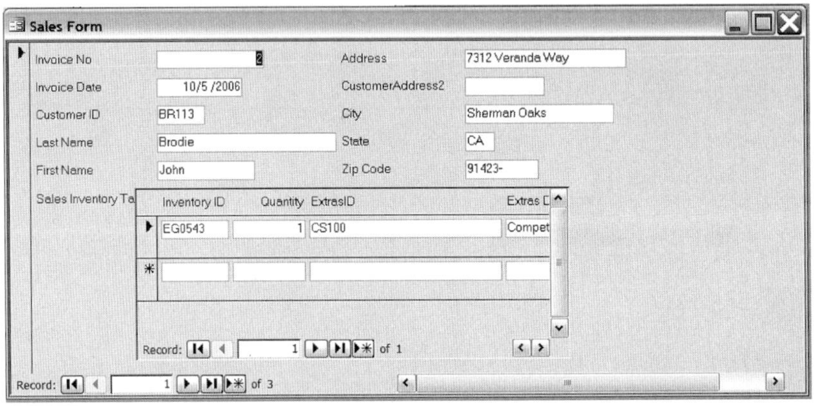

FIGURE 4-11

Since this information will be returned automatically by the database once the **CustomerID** has been entered, we can consolidate the information and make the form more user-friendly.

18. Return to the Design View. Note that the Sales Form contains a subform (the Sales Inventory Table Subform). Right-click on the Sales Form's Form Selector (the black square in the upper left corner of the form where the two rulers meet) and click on Properties in the pull-down menu (or, alternatively, click on **View** > **Properties**). Click on the Data tab, then click on the **Build** ▦ button next to the Record Source. This opens the SQL Statement: Query Builder window. Notice that the **Sales Table** and the **Customer Table** appear at the top of the window linked by **CustomerID**. Also notice that all of the fields that we added to the form appear in the columns, called the *design grid*, at the bottom of the window.

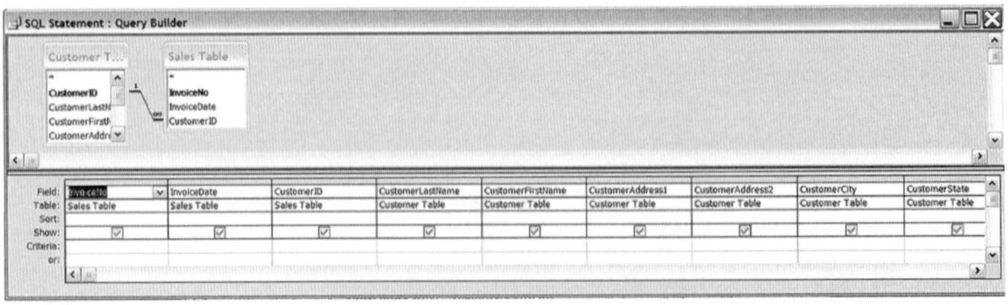

FIGURE 4-12

19. Scroll to the right of the design grid until you reach an open column. Click in the Field cell of this column and click on the **Build** ◣ icon (located on the Toolbar). This opens the Expression Builder window, which facilitates the creation of new fields in a query. Double-click on the Tables selection in the far left lower window and select the **Customer Table**.

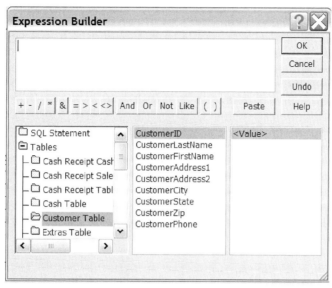

FIGURE 4-13

20. We are going to create a composite address field for the customer's city, state, and zip code so that it appears in one field. Type **CustomerCompAddress:** in the upper portion of the Expression Builder window. Double-click on **CustomerCity**; click on **&**; type "**,**" (typed as an open quotation, comma, space, close quotation); click on **&**; double-click on **CustomerState**; click on **&**; type " " (typed as an open quotation, three spaces, close quotation); click on **&**; and double-click on **CustomerZip**. Remove the ≪**Expr**≫ that was automatically inserted just after the **CustomerCompAddress** field name from the expression. (Note that there may be more than one appearance of ≪**Expr**≫. You will need to remove every instance for your expression to work properly.)

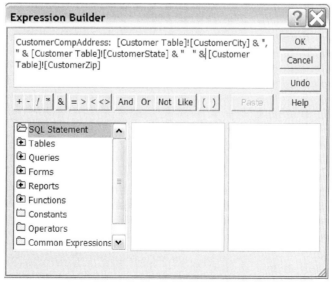

FIGURE 4-14

21. Click **OK** and click the **Run** 🔔 icon. (Note: If the **Run** icon is not visible, click on **View** > **Toolbars** > **Query Design**.)

22. Return to the design view of the SQL Statement:Query Builder. Make another composite field for the customer's name using the same process as in step 20. Put the **FirstName** field first and the **LastName** field second with a space in between (" "). Name this field **CustomerCompName**.

23. Close the Query Builder (by clicking the **X** in the upper right-hand corner) and save the query. Close the Form Properties window.

24. Delete the **LastName** and **FirstName** fields and their labels. Delete the **CustomerCity**, **CustomerState**, and **CustomerZip** fields and their labels.

25. Click on the **Field List** 🗒 icon. Scroll down and find the new **CustomerCompName** field. Click on it and drag it above the **CustomerAddress** field and drop it. Similarly, add the new **CustomerCompAddress** field below the **CustomerAddress2** field.

26. Delete the labels on the customer name and address fields by clicking on them and hitting the delete key. Be careful not to delete the fields themselves. Adjust the size of the new fields.

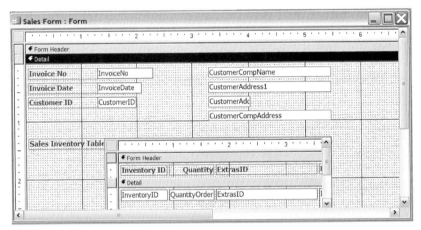

FIGURE 4-15

Since the **Customer Table** is one of the tables that data are read from in this form, we need to ensure that the user cannot write any data to the **Customer Table** in this particular application. Therefore, we now want to format the customer fields so that the user cannot change the data that is entered in these fields.

27. Place the cursor below the lower right-hand corner of the **CustomerCompAddress** field. Hold down the left mouse button and drag the cursor across all of the customer fields until you are above the upper left-hand corner of the **CustomerCompName** field.

28. We want the Customer information to automatically appear when the **CustomerID** is entered. This is called *closed-loop verification* and it is an internal control. To achieve this, right-click and select Properties to pull up the Multiple selection window. Click on the Data tab and scroll down to the Enabled line. Change it to No. Scroll to the Locked line and change it to Yes. Setting the Enable property to No results in dimming and disabling the Text Box. We don't want the Text Box to be dimmed. Therefore, we must use a combination of Locking and Disabling the Text Box. This results in leaving the data in the Text Box readable but prevents users from making changes to the value contained in the field.

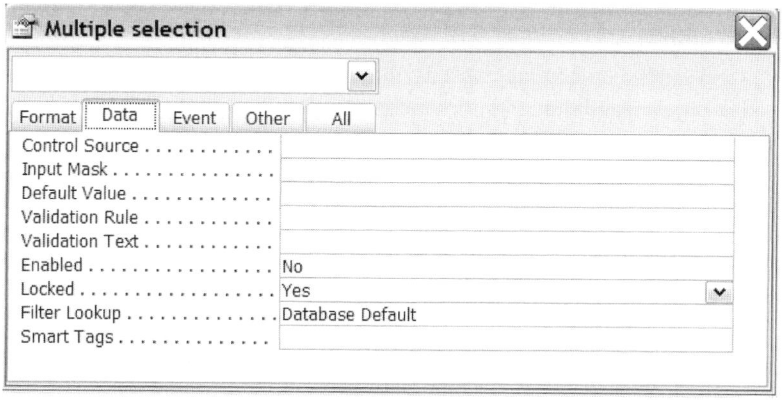

FIGURE 4-16

29. Click on the Other tab and click on Tab Stop and change it to No. This change reduces confusion for the user by ensuring that the cursor does not stop on this field while the user is inputting data into the form.

NOTE: Some versions of *Access* do not show the Enabled, Locked, or Tab Stop properties in the Multiple selection window. If this is this case, you will have to select one field at a time and repeat steps 28 and 29 for each field.

30. Click on the Format tab and click on Back Color. Click on the Build ▒▒▒ button and choose a color that will blend with the style of the form you choose. (For example, if you used Sumi Painting, you might want to choose white for the Back Color.) Click on OK. Click on Border Style and select Transparent from the pull-down menu. Close the Multiple selections window.

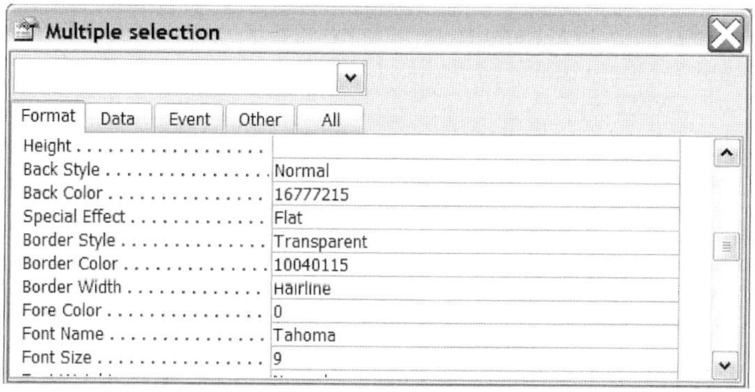

FIGURE 4-17

Now we need to work on modifying the subform.

31. Delete the label on the subform, again taking care not to delete the subform itself. Click on the subform so that the handles appear. Drag the left side of the subform to the left side of the main form. Do the same for the right side of the form.

32. Examine the labels for **Quantity** and **InventoryPrice**. Notice that they are right justified. Click on the **Quantity** label, hold the Shift key down, and click on the **InventoryPrice** label. Click on the **Align Left** ▦ to left justify these labels.

33. The **QuantityOrdered** text field and label and the **InventoryPrice** text field and label are larger than they will need to be. Adjust their size to make them smaller by clicking on each and dragging the right side of the box to the left.

34. Just as we did not want the users to change the customer's information in the main portion of the Sales Form, we do not want them to change the **InventoryDescription** or the **InventoryPrice** in the subform. Change the properties on these two fields so that the user cannot enter or change anything.

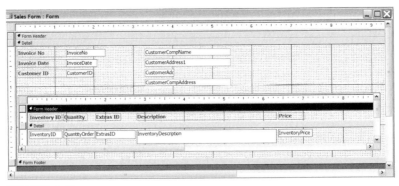

FIGURE 4-18

35. Save your form at this time.

The Sales Form: Creating a Combo Box

Since there are a limited number of extra items that can be added to customize a surfboard, we can modify the subform by adding a pull-down menu called a Combo Box from which to select these extra items.

1. The users will not need the **ExtrasID** field in the subform. Delete the **ExtrasID** field and label from the subform. You can now slide the **InventoryDescription** and **InventoryPrice** to the left so that they are next to the **QuantityOrdered**.

2. We will replace the **ExtrasDescription** and **ExtrasPrice** fields with a Combo Box. Delete the two fields, and the **ExtrasPrice** label but do not delete the label for **ExtrasDescription**. Drag the label next to the **Inventory Price** label.

3. From the Toolbox, click on the **Combo Box** ▤ icon. Drag a rectangle in the empty area in the Detail section. (Reminder: If your Toolbox disappears, you can recall it by clicking on **View** > **Toolbox**.) The Combo Box Wizard window pops up. Click **Next**.

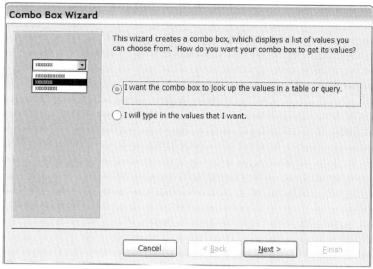

FIGURE 4-19

4. The Wizard will ask which table should provide the values for your Combo Box. Click on the **ExtrasTable** and click **Next**.

5. In the next window, select the **ExtrasDescription** and **ExtrasPrice** fields. (Make sure that *Access* automatically selected the **ExtrasID** field. If not, you will have to go back and select it manually.) Click **Next**.

6. The following window allows us to choose the order in which we want the data to be displayed in the Combo Box. Select **ExtrasDescription** and Ascending. This will result in an alphabetical display of the description in the Combo Box. Click **Next**.

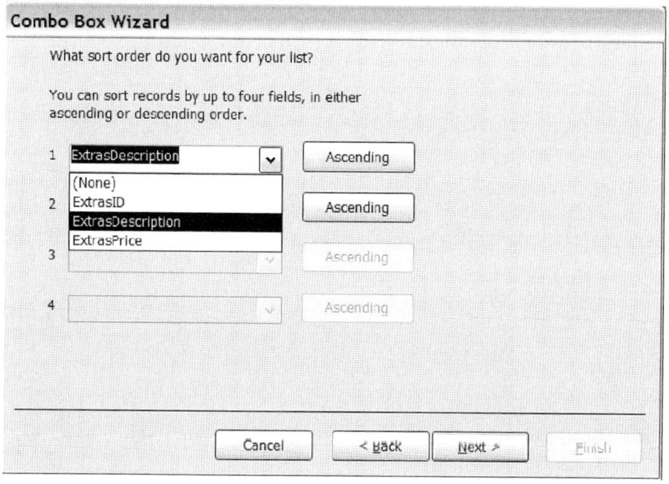

FIGURE 4-20

7. Follow the directions in the next window to adjust the column width by double-clicking on the Extras Description column and the Extras Price column and then click **Next**.

8. The next window allows us to choose how we want *Access* to store the description. We can either have it remembered for later use or stored in the **ExtrasDescription** field. Click on **Store that value in this field** and select **ExtrasID** from the pull-down menu. This binds the data that is selected in the Sales Form to the **Extras Table**. Click on **Next**.

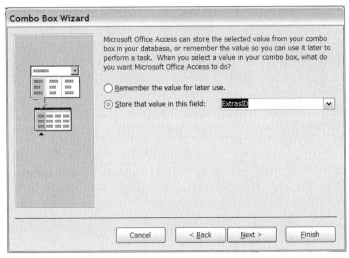

FIGURE 4-21

9. Finally, the label for the Combo Box should be **Extras Description**. Click **Finish**.

10. We already have a label for the newly created Combo Box so we can delete the new one. Be careful not to delete the Combo Box.

11. Open the form in Form View and examine your new Combo Box by clicking on the pull-down menu to ensure that all descriptions are clearly visible. The column widths can be adjusted by returning to the Design View, right-clicking on the Combo Box, and selecting Properties. The Column Widths property contains a listing of each of the column

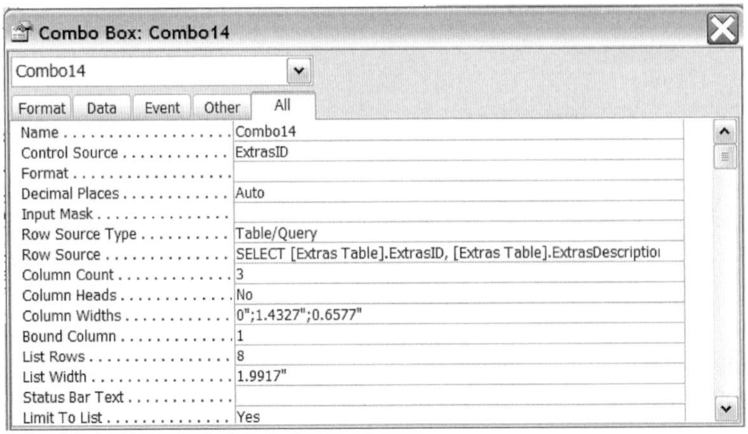

FIGURE 4-22

widths. The 0″ refers to the left margin. The next figure refers to the width of the first column, etc. Changing these amounts will adjust the width of the columns individually. Alternatively, you can drag out the length of the entire Combo Box, which will increase the width of all columns proportionately.

12. We need to extend the price of the ordered surfboard. To do this, we will have to create a new field. Right-click on the subform's selector box (at the intersection of the two rulers) and select Properties from the pull-down menu. Click on All tab. Click on the **Build** ▦ button next to the Record Source.

13. Scroll to the right of the design grid until you reach an open column. Click in the Field cell of this column and click on the **Build** ◣ icon. Type **Extension:** in the upper part of the window. Double-click on the Tables selection in the far left lower window and select the **Sales Inventory Table**. Double-click on **QuantityOrdered**. Click on * and type (. Select the **Inventory Table**. Double-click on **InventoryPrice**. Type +. Select the **Extras Table** in the far left lower window. Double-click on **ExtrasPrice**. Type). Remove the ≪**Expr**≫ that was automatically inserted just after the **Extension** field name from the expression. Click **OK** to close the Express Builder.

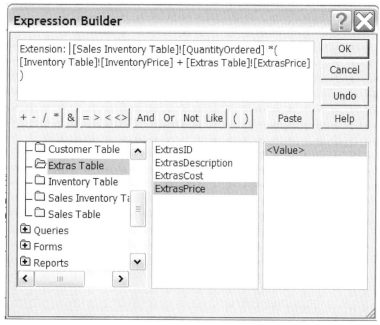

FIGURE 4-23

14. Click on **Run** ▦ and close and save the changes made to the SQL statement by clicking on the **X** in the upper right-hand corner of the Query Builder window. Close the Properties window. Click on the **Field List** icon. Scroll down and find the new **Extension** field you created. Click on it and drag it next to the **ExtrasID** field. Click on the Label for the **Extension** field. Hit **Ctrl X**. Click on the Form Header portion of the subform and hit

Ctrl V. The **Extension** field Label is now in the upper left-hand corner of the Form Header section. Drag it above the **Extension** field. Notice that the **Extension** Label has a colon after it (i.e, it reads "Extension:"). Click on the Label again and delete the colon from the label.

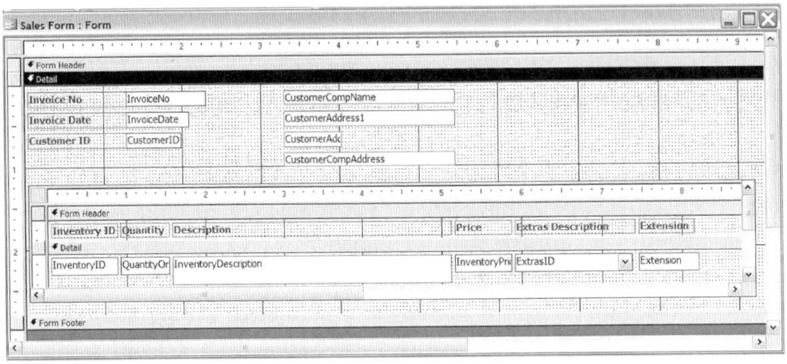

FIGURE 4-24

On occasion, a customer will order more than one surfboard. Therefore, we need to be able to arrive at a total on the **Sales Form**.

15. Stretch the **Sales Form** downward and then stretch the subform downward. Extend the Detail section of the **Sales Form**.

16. Click on the subform. Pull down the Form Footer section by placing the cursor below the Form Footer bar until the crosshairs appear and drag the cursor down approximately ½ inch.

17. Click on the Text Box **ab** icon in the Toolbox and drag a rectangle in the Form Footer section so that it is placed under the **Extension** field.

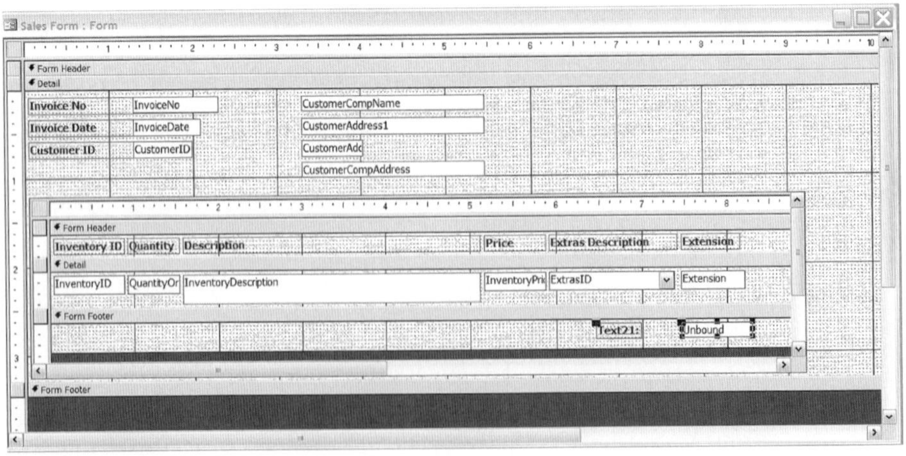

FIGURE 4-25

18. Click in the newly created Text Box and type = **Sum([Extension])**.

19. Right click on the Text Box and open the Properties window. Click on the Format tab and click on the Format property. Pull down the menu and select Currency. Close the Properties window.

20. Click on the label. Change the label to **Total**. This will sum all of the extended amounts in the Detail section of the subform.

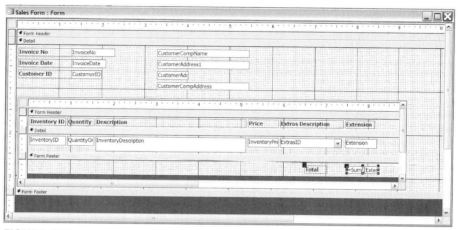

FIGURE 4-26

21. Finally, drag the top of the Detail bar down approximately ½ inch. Click on the Label **Aa** icon. Drag a rectangle in the Form Header section and type "Sales Form" in the label.

22. Close and save the form and subform.

23. Reopen the sales form. Go to a blank sales form. Create a sale for Robbie Kellerman dated October 10, 2006. He is an existing customer. His **CustomerID** is KE110. He wishes to purchase a 9′7″ King Creator surfboard. After a search of the inventory you discover that there is a red 9′7″ × 23 ⅜″ × 3 ⅜″ King Creator in stock. The **InventoryID** is KC0502. He also wishes to add a cloth design to the surfboard.

The Sales Invoice: Creating a Simple Report Based on a Query

The Sales Form we created is very useful for internal purposes; that is, it facilitates data entry. However, most customers also want to have a copy of a Sales Invoice. This requires more formatting than we can provide with the **Sales Form**. We use the **Report** object in *Access* to create the **Sales Invoice Report**. First, however, we need to gather the information necessary for the **Sales Invoice Report**. We do this by building a **Sales Invoice Query**.

1. Click on the **Queries** object. Double-click on **Create query in Design View**. (This query could also be created using the Wizard. We are using the Design View here to show this difference between the two methods.)

2. Click on the **Customer Table**, then hold down the **Ctrl** key, click on the **Extras Table**, the **Inventory Table**, the **Sales Inventory Table**, and the **Sales Table**. Click **Add**. Click **Close**.

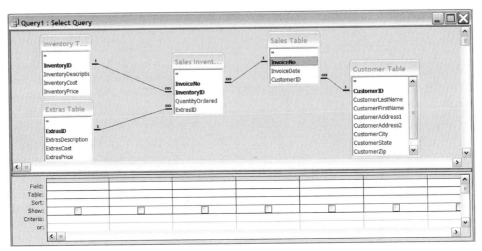

FIGURE 4-27

3. Drag all three fields from the **Sales Table** into the first three fields in the design grid.

4. Set the Sort property for **InvoiceNo** to Ascending.

5. Drag **CustomerLastName**, **CustomerFirstName**, **CustomerAddress1**, **CustomerAddress2**, **CustomerCity**, **CustomerState**, and **Customer Zip** from **Customer Table** into the next fields.

6. Drag **InventoryID**, **QuantityOrdered**, and **ExtrasID** from **Sales Inventory Table** into the next fields.

7. Drag **InventoryDescription** and **InventoryPrice** from **Inventory Table** into the next two fields.

8. Drag **ExtrasDescription** and **ExtrasPrice** from **Extras Table** into the next two fields.

9. As we did in the **Sales Form**, we need to create a **CustomerCompAddress** and **CustomerCompName**.

10. Click on the **Run** ▉ icon. Close the Query Builder and save your changes as **Sales Invoice Query**.

Now that we have gathered the information together, we are ready to create the **Sales Invoice Report**.

11. Click on the **Reports** object. Double-click on **Create report by using wizard**.

12. Select the **Sales Invoice Query**.

13. Click on >> to select all the fields. Return **CustomerLastName**, **CustomerFirstName**, **CustomerCity**, **CustomerState**, and **CustomerZip** to the **Available Fields** window. Click **Next**.

14. We will accept the data grouped as the Report Wizard has done. Click **Next**.

15. We do not need to add any additional grouping levels. Therefore, we will click **Next** in the next window.

16. Click on **InventoryID** to sort the inventory in ascending order. Click on **Next**.

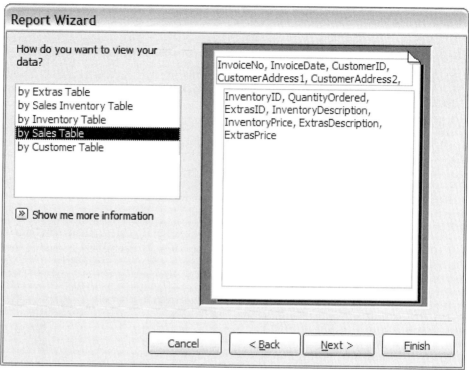

FIGURE 4-28

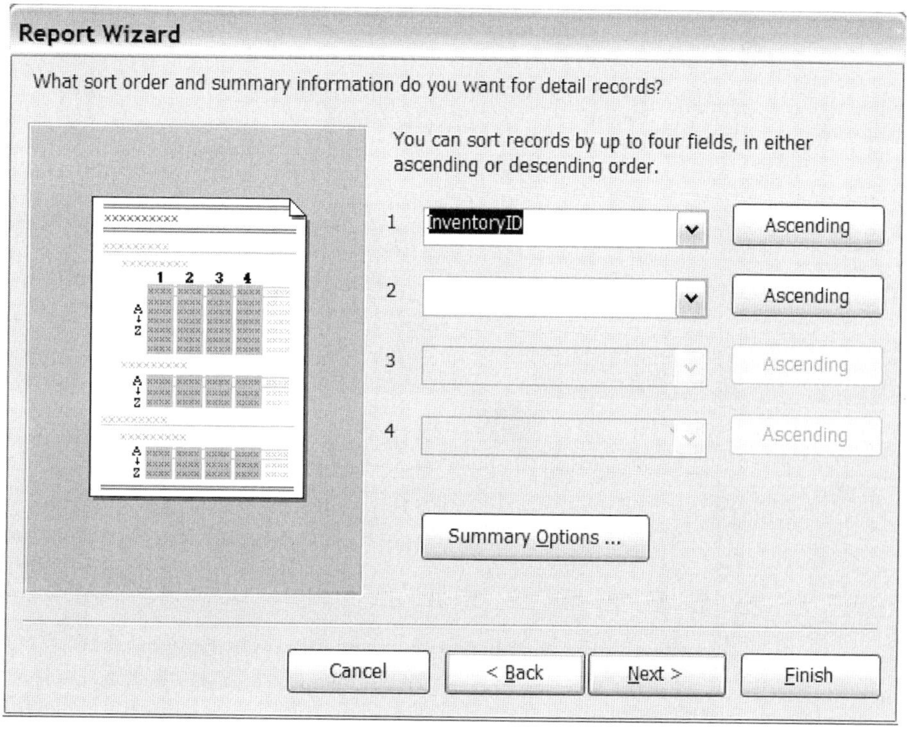

Report Wizard

What sort order and summary information do you want for detail records?

You can sort records by up to four fields, in either ascending or descending order.

1 InventoryID   ⌄   Ascending
2   ⌄   Ascending
3   ⌄   Ascending
4   ⌄   Ascending

Summary Options ...

Cancel   < Back   Next >   Finish

FIGURE 4-29

17. We need to choose the layout for the **Sales Invoice Report** in the next window. Click on each of the radial buttons to see how the layout of the invoice changes. Choose one of the layouts and click **Next**. Note that we have chosen Align Left 1 for our report.

18. We are now asked to choose a style for the Report. We have chosen the Casual style for our report. Choose one and click **Next**.

19. Change the report name to **Sales Invoice Report** and click on **Modify the report's Design**. Click **Finish**.

20. Before deciding what modifications are necessary to the **Sales Invoice Report**, we need to examine it. Click on the **View** icon.

21. We can see that we have several invoices printed on one page and many of the fields are overlapping. Click on the **View** icon again to modify the report.

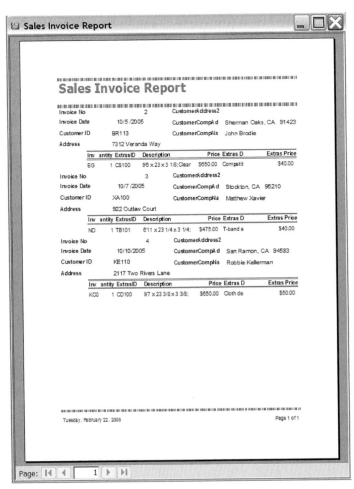

FIGURE 4-30

Notice that the title of the report "Sales Invoice Report" appears only once for all of the invoices. The title is in the Report Header section of the report. The Report Header section is used to place information at the beginning of a report. We want the title to appear at the beginning of every Sales Invoice. Therefore, we need to move the label control and the line object from the Report header section to the InvoiceNo Header section.

22. Click on the top of the Detail section bar and drag it downward about 1¼ inch.

23. Before we begin to move any labels or any controls, notice that the width of the Report is 6½ inches. It is important that you do not exceed this width. If you do, *Access* will place labels and controls on a second page. Now place your cursor to the lower right of all the labels and controls in the InvoiceNo Header section and drag it to the upper left so that you select all of the labels and controls in that section. Drag them downward so that they are once more aligned with the top of the Detail section bar.

24. Select the label control and line object from the Report Header section in the same way, by placing your cursor to the lower right and dragging it to the upper left. Drag them to the InvoiceNo Header section.

25. Select **View** and deselect the Report Header/Footer section from the menu to delete this section.

26. Select **View** again and deselect the Page Header/Footer section from the menu to delete this section. If asked, click the **Yes** button to confirm the deletion.

27. Since this is the Sales Invoice we are giving to our customers, we do not need the word report to be included. Edit the title by clicking on it and deleting the word "Report."

28. We also need to rearrange the customer information so that it appears in the proper order (**CustomerCompName**, **CustomerAddress1**, **CustomerAddress2**, **CustomerCompAddress**), with all fields on the right side of the invoice. Remove the labels for these fields.

29. To make the form more user-friendly, we can adjust the length of the **InvoiceNo** and **InvoiceDate** fields.

30. Now we need to work on the spacing of the labels and related controls so they no longer overlap. We can delete the **ExtrasID** field since we do not need that. In addition, we will need to leave space on the right side since we do not have a field to extend the price.

In creating space for all of the fields, we can increase the depth of the description fields.

31. Now we are ready to extend the price of each surfboard purchased. Click on the Text Box ![ab] icon and draw a rectangle in the space you have made at the right of the Detail section. Delete the Label. Right click inside the Text Box and click on Properties. Click on the All tab. In the Control Source property, type: = **[QuantityOrdered]** **(**[InventoryPrice]** + **[ExtrasPrice]**)*. Change the Name property to **ReportExtension** and change the Format property to Currency. Close the Properties window.

32. Click on the **Label** ![Aa] icon and draw a rectangle in the empty space in the InvoiceNo Header section. Type "Extension" in this rectangle.

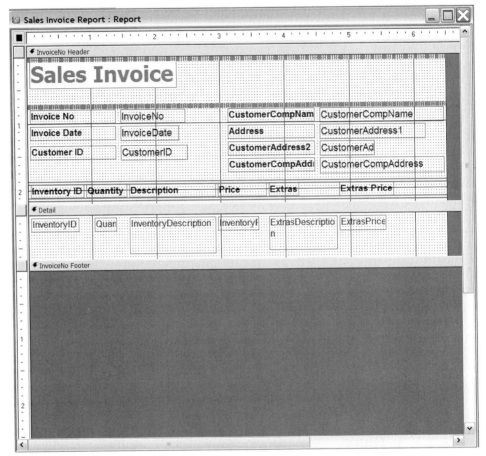

FIGURE 4-31

Text Box: ReportExtension	
ReportExtension	
Format	Data	Event	Other	All

Name	ReportExtension
Control Source	=[QuantityOrdered]*([InventoryPrice]+[ExtrasPrice])
Format	Currency
Decimal Places	Auto
Input Mask	
Visible	Yes
Vertical	No
Hide Duplicates	No
Can Grow	No
Can Shrink	No
Running Sum	No
Left	5.7083"
Top	0.0417"
Width	0.6667"
Height	0.2083"
Back Style	Transparent
Back Color	16777215

FIGURE 4-32

33. We still need a total for the **Sales Invoice**. Right click on the Detail section bar. Click on the **Sorting and Grouping** option. Note that we are already grouping on the InvoiceNo Header.

	Build Event...
	Sorting and Grouping
	Paste
	Fill/Back Color ▶
	Ruler
	Grid
	Toolbox
	Page Header/Footer
	Report Header/Footer
	Properties

FIGURE 4-33

34. Change the grouping option on InvoiceNo Footer from No to Yes. Close the Sorting and Grouping window.

Sorting and Grouping

Field/Expression	Sort Order	
InvoiceNo	Ascending	
InventoryID	Ascending	

Group Properties

Group Header	Yes	Select a field or type an expression to sort or group on
Group Footer	Yes	
Group On	Each Value	
Group Interval	1	
Keep Together	No	

FIGURE 4-34

35. Stretch the newly created footer downward approximately ¼ inch. Create a Text Box in the InvoiceNo Footer below the **ReportExtension** field you created in the Detail section. Right-click on the Text Box and click on Properties. Click on the All tab. Type = **Sum([QuantityOrdered]*([InventoryPrice] + [ExtrasPrice]))** in the Control Source of this box. Change the Name property to **InvoiceTotal** and change the Format property to Currency.

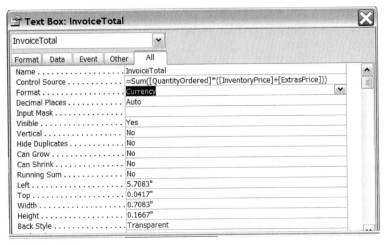

FIGURE 4-35

36. Click on the Label attached to the Text Box and change it to **Invoice Total**.

37. The last step is to make sure we print only one invoice per page. Right click on the InvoiceNo Footer, click on Properties, and click on the Format tab. Change the Force New Page property to After Section. Close the Section property window.

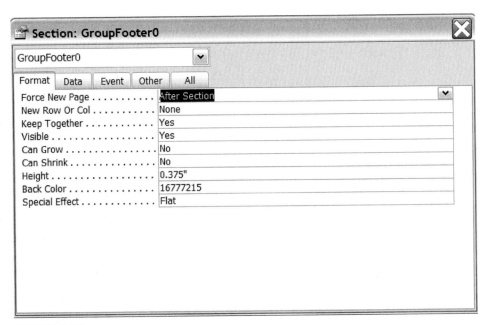

FIGURE 4-36

38. Before you close and save the **Sales Invoice Report** switch to the Print View to be sure that the Sales Invoice is ready.

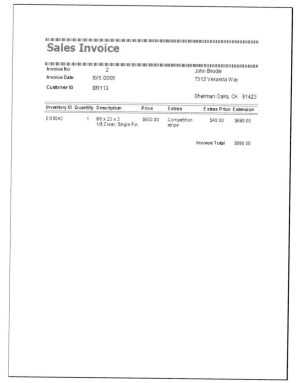

FIGURE 4-37

Queries with Simple Criteria

There are various types of queries that provide useful information in the Sales/Collection Business Process. We created some of these queries while building the Sales Form in the previous exercise. In addition, both internal and external users often need to query the database to obtain information. For example, Dan Tragg may wish to obtain a list of each inventory item and its selling price to determine whether they are low on any particular type of surfboard. To obtain this information, we would use a Select Query. A select query is the most commonly used type of query. It retrieves rows of data from one or more tables and displays the results in a dynaset. The select query can be enhanced to group records and calculate sums, averages, and other totals.

To obtain the inventory list for Tragg's Custom Surfboard is relatively easy and requires the use of only one table.

1. Click on the **Queries** object. Click on **Create query in Design view**. Click on **Inventory Table** in the Show Table window, click **Add** and click **Close**.

2. Drag **InventoryID**, **InventoryDescription**, and **InventoryPrice** into the first three columns of the design grid.

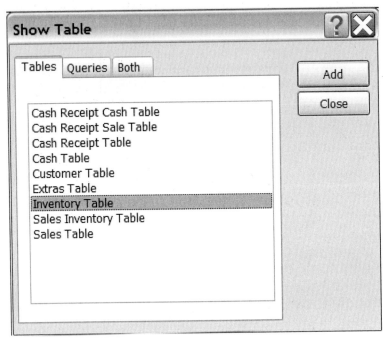

FIGURE 4-38

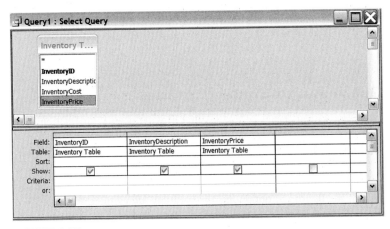

FIGURE 4-39

3. Click on Ascending in the Sort property for the **InventoryID** field and click on the **Run** icon.

4. Click on the **Design View** icon.

We can refine this query by searching for inventory on hand that are priced less than $675.00. This utilizes the Criteria property in the design grid.

5. Type < 675.00 in the Criteria property for the **InventoryPrice** field and click on the **Run** icon again.

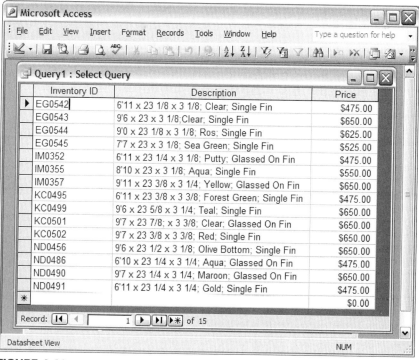

FIGURE 4-40

Inventory ID	Description	Price
EG0542	6'11 x 23 1/8 x 3 1/8; Clear; Single Fin	$475.00
EG0543	9'6 x 23 x 3 1/8;Clear; Single Fin	$650.00
EG0544	9'0 x 23 1/8 x 3 1/8; Ros; Single Fin	$625.00
EG0545	7'7 x 23 x 3 1/8; Sea Green; Single Fin	$525.00
IM0352	6'11 x 23 1/4 x 3 1/8; Putty; Glassed On Fin	$475.00
IM0355	8'10 x 23 x 3 1/8; Aqua; Single Fin	$550.00
IM0356	10'2 x 23 5/8 x 3 5/8; Navy; Single Fin	$675.00
IM0357	9'11 x 23 3/8 x 3 1/4; Yellow; Glassed On Fin	$650.00
KC0495	6'11 x 23 3/8 x 3 3/8; Forest Green; Single Fin	$475.00
KC0499	9'6 x 23 5/8 x 3 1/4; Teal; Single Fin	$650.00
KC0501	9'7 x 23 7/8; x 3 3/8; Clear; Glassed On Fin	$650.00
KC0502	9'7 x 23 3/8 x 3 3/8; Red; Single Fin	$650.00
KC0503	10'9 x 23 5/8 x 3 3/8; Black; Glassed On Fin	$700.00
ND0456	9'6 x 23 1/2 x 3 1/8; Olive Bottom; Single Fin	$650.00
ND0486	6'10 x 23 1/4 x 3 1/4; Aqua; Glassed On Fin	$475.00
ND0487	10'0 x 23 5/8 x 3 3/8; Apple Green; Single Fin	$700.00
ND0488	10'6 x 23 5/8 x 3 3/8; Clear; Single Fin	$700.00
ND0489	10'4 x 23 1/2 x 3 3/8; Tan; Glassed On Fin	$675.00
ND0490	9'7 x 23 1/4 x 3 1/4; Maroon; Glassed On Fin	$650.00
ND0491	6'11 x 23 1/4 x 3 1/4; Gold; Single Fin	$475.00
*		$0.00

Record: 1 of 20

FIGURE 4-41

Inventory ID	Description	Price
EG0542	6'11 x 23 1/8 x 3 1/8; Clear; Single Fin	$475.00
EG0543	9'6 x 23 x 3 1/8;Clear; Single Fin	$650.00
EG0544	9'0 x 23 1/8 x 3 1/8; Ros; Single Fin	$625.00
EG0545	7'7 x 23 x 3 1/8; Sea Green; Single Fin	$525.00
IM0352	6'11 x 23 1/4 x 3 1/8; Putty; Glassed On Fin	$475.00
IM0355	8'10 x 23 x 3 1/8; Aqua; Single Fin	$550.00
IM0357	9'11 x 23 3/8 x 3 1/4; Yellow; Glassed On Fin	$650.00
KC0495	6'11 x 23 3/8 x 3 3/8; Forest Green; Single Fin	$475.00
KC0499	9'6 x 23 5/8 x 3 1/4; Teal; Single Fin	$650.00
KC0501	9'7 x 23 7/8; x 3 3/8; Clear; Glassed On Fin	$650.00
KC0502	9'7 x 23 3/8 x 3 3/8; Red; Single Fin	$650.00
ND0456	9'6 x 23 1/2 x 3 1/8; Olive Bottom; Single Fin	$650.00
ND0486	6'10 x 23 1/4 x 3 1/4; Aqua; Glassed On Fin	$475.00
ND0490	9'7 x 23 1/4 x 3 1/4; Maroon; Glassed On Fin	$650.00
ND0491	6'11 x 23 1/4 x 3 1/4; Gold; Single Fin	$475.00
*		$0.00

Record: 1 of 15

6. Close and save query as **Inventory Query**.

Queries with Multiple Values

A Parameter Query is one that prompts the user for the query criteria for retrieving records. These criteria can be single-valued or multi-valued. In addition, the criteria can be entered as absolute values or as wildcards. Assume that a company has a calendar year-end. We can query for all sales greater than $650.00 between January 1, 2006 and December 31, 2006. We could also create the query by using wildcards for the dates. In this case, the query would substitute variables such as "BeginDate" and "BSDate." In this parameter query, *Access* then prompts the user for the appropriate values.

Assume that Dan Tragg wants to view his Cash Receipts for October. We can easily create a query that will isolate those cash receipts.

1. Click on the **Queries** object. Click on **Create query in design view**. Click on the **Cash Receipt Table** to add it to the upper part of the Query window. Hold down the **Ctrl** key and click on the **Cash Receipt Sale Table** and click on **Add**. Close the Show Table window.

2. Drag the **CashReceiptID** and the **CRDate** fields from the **Cash Receipt Table** into the first two columns of the design grid. Drag the **AmountApplied** field from the **Cash Receipt Sale Table** into the third column of the design grid.

3. Click on the Totals ∑ icon. Pull down the menu under the Total property for the **CRDate**. Note that there are various mathematical functions (including Sum and Average) that we could choose here. However, these are not appropriate for a date field. Scroll down to the bottom of the menu. The "Where" function will allow us to set the criteria for the date. Change the Total property for the **CRDate** field to "Where."

4. In the Criteria property of the **CRDate** field, type **Between [BeginDate] and [EndDate]**.

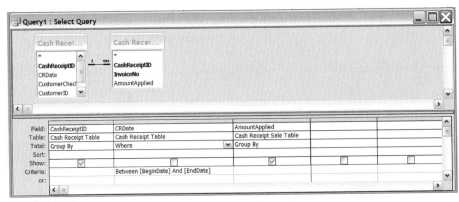

FIGURE 4-42

5. Click on the **Run** ! icon.

6. Type 10/1/2006 in the prompt for the BeginDate. Click **OK**.

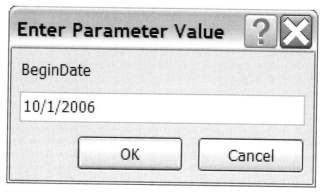

FIGURE 4-43

7. Type 10/31/2006 when prompted for the EndDate.

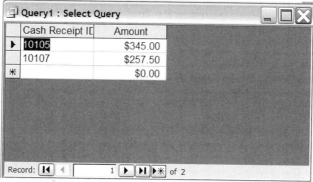

FIGURE 4-44

8. Save the query as **Monthly Cash Receipts Query**.

KEY TERMS

business process
closed loop verification
Combo Box

design grid
Select Query
Parameter Query

Sales/Collection business
process

QUESTIONS AND PROBLEMS FOR REVIEW

MULTIPLE-CHOICE QUESTIONS

4.1 To convert a conceptual model with a maximum cardinality relationship of "many to many" into relationship database tables, you must
  (a) Create a foreign key in one of the tables to link the two tables
  (b) Create a relation with no attributes of its own

(c) Create a separate table with a concatenated primary key comprised of the primary keys from both entity tables

(e) Many to many relationships cannot be represented in *Access.*

4.2 A control in which you can type a value or can click on a pull-down menu to display a list and then select an item from that list is called a

    (a) Control Box

    (b) Text Box

    (c) Combo Box

    (d) Source Box

    (e) None of the above

4.3 A query that displays its own dialog box prompting the user for information for retrieving records is called a(n)

    (a) Select Query

    (b) Parameter Query

    (c) Crosstab Query

    (d) Action Query

    (e) None of the above

4.4 To ensure that users cannot enter data in certain fields, the Locked and Enabled properties should be set to

    (a) Locked = Yes, Enabled = No

    (b) Locked = Yes, Enabled = Yes

    (c) Locked = No, Enabled = Yes

    (d) Locked = No, Enabled = No

PROBLEMS

4.1 Create a query for Tragg's Custom Surfboards to sum the cash receipts (grand total for the year) as of December 31, 2006. Save the query so that you can easily provide them with this information for other months in the future.

4.2 Alter the query created in Problem 4.1 to sum the cash receipts for each customer as of December 31, 2006. Save the query.

4.3 Tragg's Custom Surfboards needs to know how many inventory items were sold during the month of October 2006. Create the query to provide this information. Save the query.

4.4 Tragg's also wants to know the cost of inventory sold during the month of October 2006. Create the query to provide this information. Save the query.

4.5 Tragg's has asked you for the total sales (in dollars) for the month of October 2006. Save this query so that you can easily provide them with this information for other months in the future.

4.6 Create a Daily Cash Report for Tragg's Custom Surfboards showing the customer number, invoice number, date, customer check number, and amount of payment.

CHAPTER 5

ACQUISITION/PAYMENT BUSINESS PROCESS

INTRODUCTION

The Acquisition/Payment business process is often referred to as the *expenditure transaction cycle*. The Acquisition/Payment business process often includes the instigation events (i.e., purchase requisitions), the mutual commitment events (i.e., purchase orders), the economic increment events (i.e., purchase of goods or services), and the economic decrement event (i.e., the cash disbursement). We might also see an economic increment reversal event (i.e., the purchase return).

To model the Acquisition/Payment business process in a database, it will be useful to create more complex forms, reports, and queries. After completing this chapter, you should be able to use *Microsoft Access* to:

- Create an AutoNumber starting at any number you wish.
- Create an append query to add records in a dynaset to an existing table.
- Create queries involving multiple tables, derived column values, and expressions.
- Create queries that can handle null values.
- Create forms and reports using multiple tables and queries.

ACQUISITION/PAYMENT PROCESS OVERVIEW

Basic Concepts and Definitions

We refer to Figure 1-3 and see that the expenditure cycle interfaces with the conversion cycle, the financing cycle, and the financial reporting system. The financial reporting system interfaces with the expenditure cycle and the payroll cycle. Extending this to the framework of business processes, goods and services are acquired by a company as a result of the Acquisition/Payment process. The Acquisition/Payment process delivers those goods and services either to the Sales/Collection process for sale and subsequent cash collection or to the Conversion Process for further processing, which in turn delivers them to the Sales/Collection Process for sale and subsequent cash collection. Once the cash is collected, it is made available to the Financing process and, in turn, is used to pay for the goods and services acquired by the Acquisition/Payment process. For this to happen, the Acquisition/Payment process must include at least one economic event that transfers goods and services into the company (i.e., an increment event) and at least one economic event that transfers out the cash (i.e., a decrement event). The Acquisition/Payment process for all firms is similar regardless of whether the firm is engaged in manufacturing, in service, or in retail.

Tragg's Custom Surfboards

Additional Background Dan Tragg insists on using only the highest quality materials in the manufacturing of his surfboards. Tragg's uses a list of approved suppliers with whom they have established a good relationship over the years. For example, they obtain their blanks (the molds for their surfboards) from one of two vendors, SeaFoam or Clarke Foam. These companies manufacture blanks that are near perfect in density from deck to core without compromising weight. In addition, they have a wide variety of blanks. The result is that Tragg's incurs much less waste when shaping the surfboard into one of its styles.

The boards are laminated with Volan fiberglass, which is a flat-weave fiberglass cloth that resists dings. This finish also makes the boards water tight, stronger, and more durable. They outsource the application of most of the Volan fiberglass finish to a well-established glasser, Austad Glassing. Pigments and other supplies are obtained through several suppliers with whom Tragg's has been dealing over a period of years.

Model the Expenditure Cycle Using REA As we begin modeling the expenditure cycle using the REA diagram, we will focus our discussion on the purchase of inventory (i.e., the blanks, or molds, for each style of surfboard sold). Obviously, there are expenditures for goods other than inventory. For example, there are expenditures for fixed assets, for miscellaneous supplies, and for services. Similarly, there are items (i.e., fixed assets and miscellaneous supplies) that are received other than inventory. For simplicity's sake, we have chosen not to represent those in the REA diagram so that you can focus on the process of purchasing, receiving, and paying for inventory.

Since the blanks are purchased for each style of surfboard sold, Tragg's is able to use only one inventory table to record the inventory for all of its stock, both production and retail. The blanks are purchased when a production supervisor recognizes a need for inventory. The supervisor goes to his or her terminal and completes a Purchase Order Form online. This is done by selecting the vendor, as well as the inventory and amounts to be ordered. The order can be for one type of blank or for several types. The Purchase Order Form is reviewed by a Purchasing Agent. If it is approved, a Purchase Order Report is prepared, printed, and mailed to SeaFoam or Clarke Foam.

The goods are received and counted by the receiving clerk. The receiving clerk enters the date, the PO Number, and the Supplier's Invoice Number in the top portion of the form. In addition, the clerk must enter the Inventory ID number and the quantity received in the form.

If the order is in agreement with the Purchase Order, it is scheduled for payment. A separate receiving report will be completed for each Purchase Order; however, if any goods are backordered (which happens on rare occasions), Tragg's may have to complete more than one Receiving Report for a Purchase Order. Tragg's sometimes pays for more than one invoice (receipt of inventory) with each check (cash disbursement). In addition, on occasion they have placed very large orders and have paid for those orders in installments.

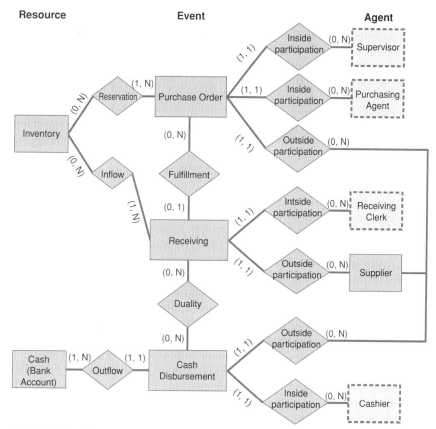

FIGURE 5-1 Basic REA Diagram for Tragg's Custom Surfboards Expenditure Cycle

Create a Relational Database for Tragg's Following the REA Diagram

Based on Figure 5-1, Tragg's table structure for the Acquisition/Payment Business Process can be represented as follows (for the sake of simplicity, we are not including those tables that are denoted by a dotted line):

Cash Table (CashAcctNo, AcctType)

Inventory Table (InventoryID, InventoryDescription, InventoryCost, InventoryPrice)

Cash Disbursement Receiving Table (CashDisbursementID, RecRptNo, AmountApplied)

PO Inventory Table (PONo, InventoryID, POQuantityOrdered)

Cash Disbursement Table (CashDisbursementID, CDDate, SupplierID, CashAcctNo)

Purchase Order Table (PONo, PODate, SupplierID)

Supplier Table (SupplierID, SupplierName, SupplierAddress1, SupplierAddress2, SupplierCity, SupplierState, SupplierZip, SupplierPhone)

Receiving Report Table (RecRptNo, RecRptDate, PONo, SupplierInvNo)

Receiving Inventory Table (RecRptNo, InventoryID, QuantityReceived)

Tragg's Relational Database Using Access

Open the Chapter 5 database for Tragg's Custom Surfboards. Again note that all the tables, some relationships, and some forms have already been created for the Acquisition/ Payment business process. Take some time to examine the tables, forms, and the relationships that have been created thus far.

The Purchase Order Table and The Append Query

Recall that in Chapter 4, when we created the **Sales Form** and began entering data, the **InvoiceNo** field Data Type was set as AutoNumber. It began numbering the **Sales Forms** at 1 and continued forward from there. We do not have to begin numbering all of our forms at 1. We can be numbering our forms at any number of our choosing. Therefore, let's assume that Tragg's would like to begin numbering the **Purchase Order Forms** at 1000.

Open the Tragg's Custom Surfboard database for Chapter 5 and take some time to acquaint yourself with the **Purchase Order Table** at this time. Notice that we have not yet set the Primary Key for this table. This is because we will be setting a default value to begin the number of the **Purchase Order Forms** and we cannot do this if the table prevents null values in the primary key field. In other words, the Required Field property cannot be set to **Yes**, and the Indexed field property cannot be set to **Yes (No Duplicates)**. Therefore, we have not yet set the Primary Key.

1. Close the **Purchase Order Table**.

2. Click on **Create Table in Design View**.

3. Type **PONo** in the Field Name and choose Number as the Data Type.

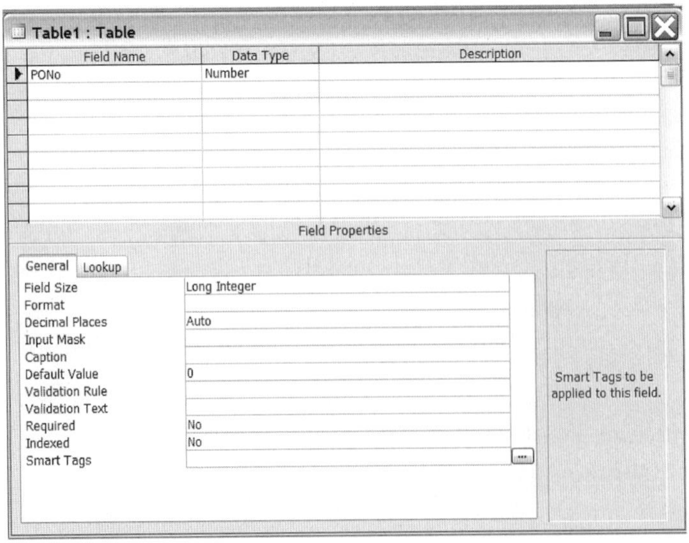

FIGURE 5-2

4. Close and save the table as **Temp PO Table**. The following window will appear, asking you if you want to create a primary key. Click **No**.

FIGURE 5-3

5. Open the **Temp PO Table**. In the Datasheet View, we will enter a value in the Number of field that is one (1) less than the starting value we want for the AutoNumber field. In other words, since we want the **Purchase Order Form** to begin at 1000, we will enter 999 in this field.

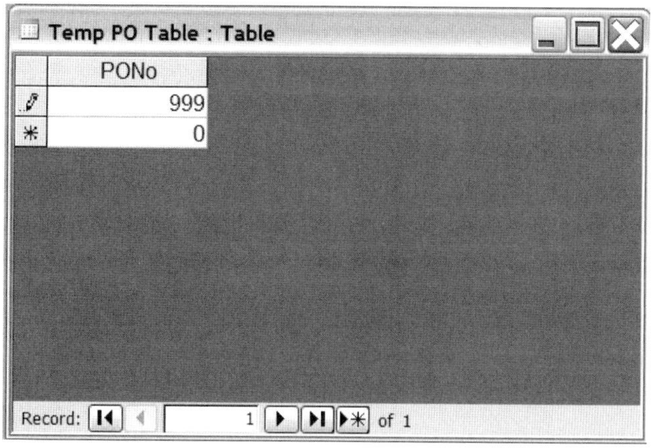

FIGURE 5-4

6. Close the table.

7. Click on the **Queries** object and double-click on **Create query in Design view**.

8. Scroll down in the Show Table window and double-click **Temp PO Table**. Close the Show Table window.

9. Click on the **Query Type** icon. (Note: If this icon is not in the menu, click on **View** > **Toolbars** > **Query Design** to pull it up.) Click on the **Append Query** . An Append Query adds a group of records from one or more tables to the end of one or more tables. We want *Access* to add the **PONumber** automatically each time a new Purchase Order is created. In the Table Name field, select the **Purchase Order Table**. Click **OK**.

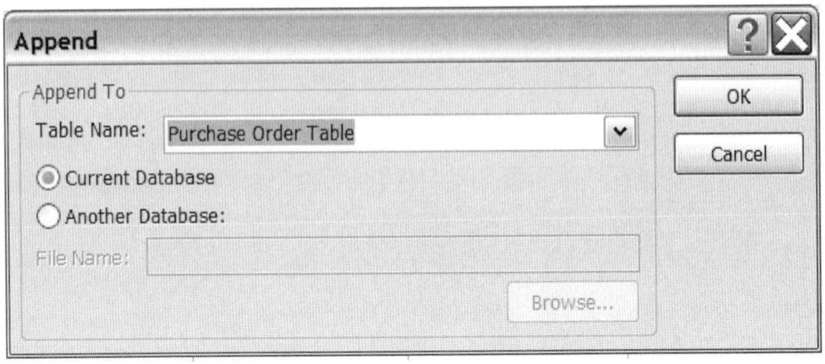

FIGURE 5-5

10. In the upper portion of the Query window, drag **PONo** from **Temp PO Table** to the first field in the design grid. Since the field we selected has the same name as the Primary Key in the **Purchase Order Table**, *Access* will automatically fill the matching name in the **Append To** row.

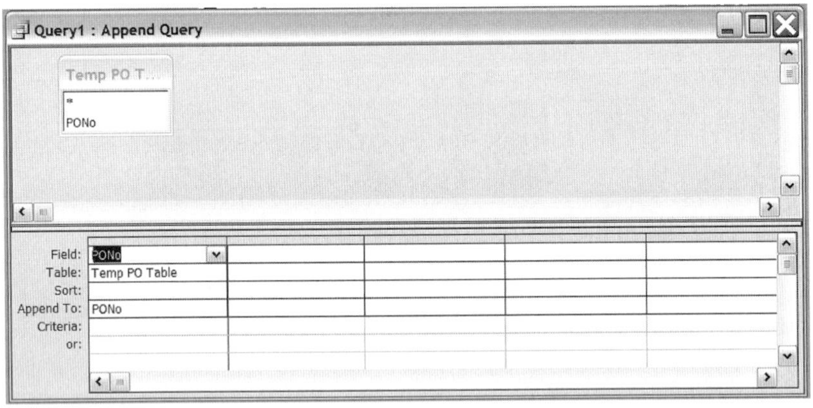

FIGURE 5-6

11. Click on the **Run** [■] icon. A window will appear informing you that you are about to append 1 row. Click **Yes**.

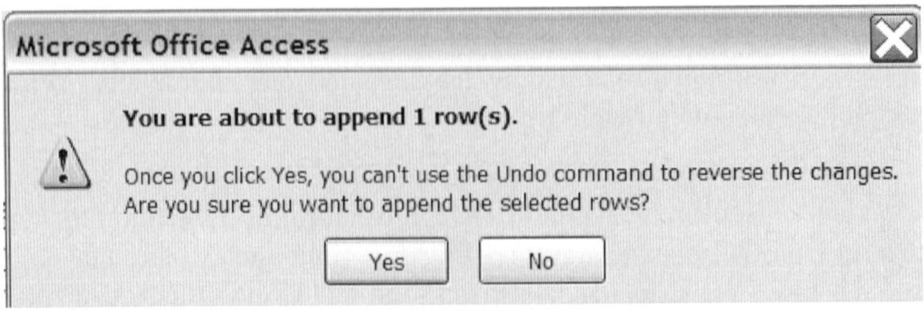

FIGURE 5-7

12. Click on the Datasheet View ▓ icon to be sure that the **Append Query** worked satisfactorily. You should see one record in the **PONo** field with 999 in it.

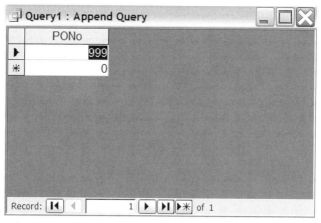

FIGURE 5-8

13. Close and save the query as **PO No Query**.

14. Click on the **Tables** object and delete the temporary table, **Temp PO Table**, since we no longer need this table.

15. Open **Purchase Order Table** in **Design** view. Set **PONo** as the Primary Key. Close and save the changes to the table.

16. Double-click on the **Purchase Order Table**. You will see that 999 has now been set in the **PONo** field and the AutoNumber is ready to begin the next Purchase Order at 1000.

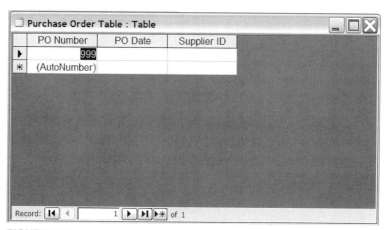

FIGURE 5-9

The Relationships: Making the Necessary Linkages

1. Examine Figure 5-1 carefully. Now that we have created the Primary Key for the **Purchase Order Table**, we need to create the necessary relationships. Click on the Relationships 🔲 icon to open the window. Notice that we need to add the **Purchase Order Table** and the **PO Inventory Table**. Click on the **Show Table** 🔲 icon.

2. Click on the **PO Inventory Table**, hold down the **Ctrl** key, and click on the **Purchase Order Table**. Click on the **Add** key and click **Close**.

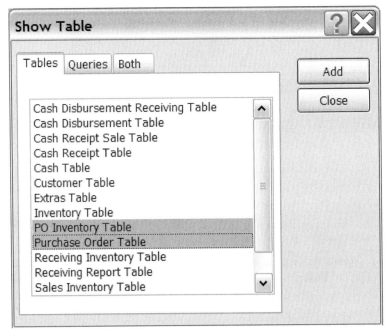

FIGURE 5-10

3. Make the necessary linkages by dragging the primary keys to their foreign keys in the appropriate tables. Recall that when you do this, the Edit Relationships window appears. Click on the **Enforce Referential Integrity** button.

4. Create the other two necessary relationships.

5. Close the Relationships window and save the changes.

The Purchase Order Form

Now that the Relationships have been created, we are ready to begin creating the **Purchase Order Form**. As we found with the **Sales Form**, this form will require the use of several tables. We will need to be able to read from the **Supplier Table** to obtain supplier

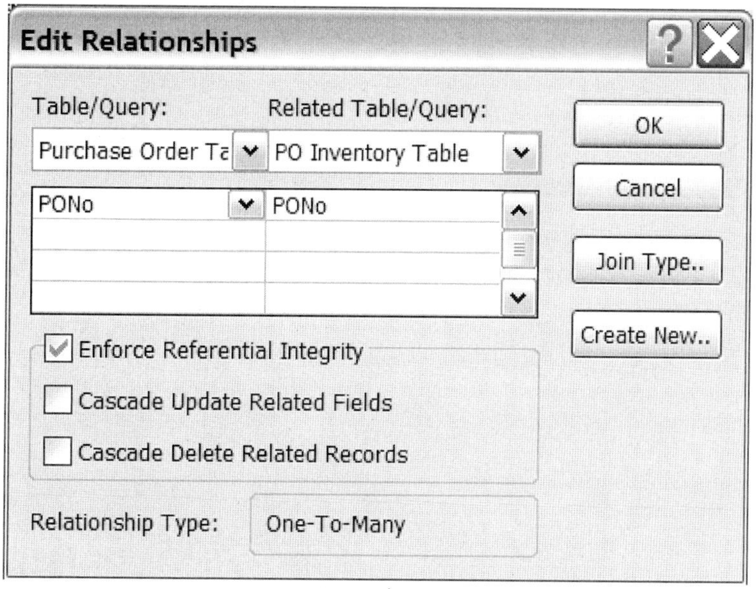

FIGURE 5-11

information and from the **Inventory Table** to obtain the description and cost of the items ordered. We will need to be able to write to the **Purchase Order Table** to enter the PO Number, date, and supplier information and to the **PO Inventory Table** to list the required Inventory IDs and quantities.

1. Click on the **Forms** object and double-click on **Create form by using wizard**.

2. From the Tables/Queries pull-down menu, select the **Purchase Order Table** and select all three fields for inclusion in the form by clicking ≫.

NOTE: After you select fields for inclusion from this table and from tables in the future, it is important to be sure that the last field is highlighted in the Selected Fields window. If it is not, the fields will be out of order when the form is created and you will have to rearrange them!

3. Select the **Supplier Table** and select **SupplierName** for inclusion in the form.

4. Select the **PO Inventory Table** and, as before, select **InventoryID** and **POQuantityOrdered** for inclusion.

5. Select **Inventory Table** and select **InventoryDescription** and **InventoryCost** for inclusion in the form.

6. Click the **Next** button. The Form Wizard automatically suggests a layout for the **Purchase Order Form** (containing fields from the **Purchase Order Table** and the **Supplier Table**) with a subform (containing the fields from the **PO Inventory Table** and the **Inventory Table**).

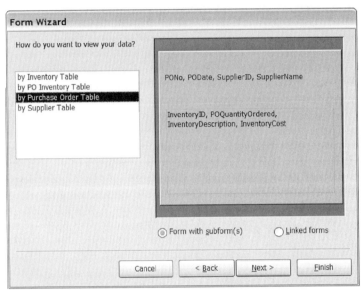

FIGURE 5-12

Accept the layout by clicking the **Next** button.

7. Select the Tabular layout for the subform in the next window and click **Next**. Select a style for your form and click **Next**. Change the name of the form to **Purchase Order Form** (leave the name of the subform alone). Click on **Modify the form's design**. Click on **Finish**.

8. Stretch the form out to 7½ inches.

9. Delete the label for the **SupplierName** field. Drag the Text Box for **SupplierName** so that it is opposite the **SupplierID** Text Box.

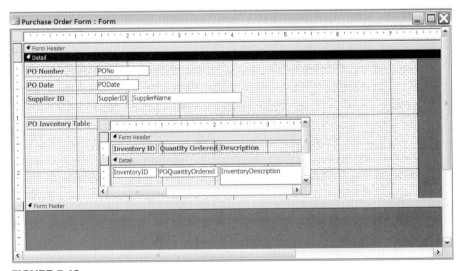

FIGURE 5-13

10. We want Supplier Name to automatically appear when the user types a Supplier ID into the Purchase Order Form. Recall from Chapter 4 that this provides us with closed-loop verification. Therefore, you should format the **SupplierName** so that the user cannot change the data that is entered in this field in the same manner as we protected the customer fields in the **Sales Form** in Chapter 4.

11. Right-click on the **SupplierName** Text Box and select Properties. Click on the Data tab and scroll down to the Enabled line. Change it to No. Scroll to the Locked line and change it to Yes. Click on the Other tab and click on Tab Stop and change it to No.

12. Click on the Format tab and click on Back Color. Click on the Build ▓▓▓ button and choose a color that will blend with the style of the form you choose. Click on **OK**. Click on Border Style and select Transparent from the pull-down menu. Close the Properties window.

The subform also needs to be modified. We need to stretch it out to see the entire form.

13. Delete the label on the subform. Click on the subform so that the handles appear. Drag the left side of the subform to the left side of the main form. Drag the right side of the subform to the right side of the main form.

14. Scroll to the right of the subform and shrink the size of the **InventoryCost** Text Box and Label. Examine the label for **InventoryCost**. Notice that it is right-justified. Click on the Align Left ▤ to left justify this label.

15. Just as we did not want the users to change the customer's information in the main portion of the **Purchase Order Form**, we do not want them to change the **InventoryDescription** or the **InventoryCost** in the subform. Change the properties on these two fields so that the user cannot enter or change anything.

16. Create a label for the form in the Form Header section entitled **Purchase Order Form**.

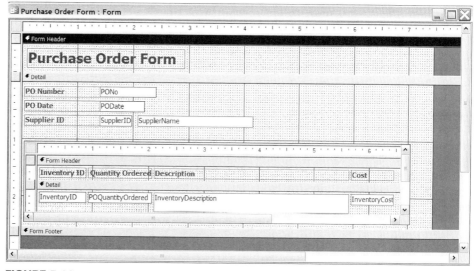

FIGURE 5-14

17. Save and close your form at this time.

18. Enter the following Purchase Orders at this time.

- PO No. 1000
  Vendor: SeaFoam (SEA100)
  Date: 9/15/2006
  Inventory Ordered:
  　　　40 Egotists blanks (EG0000)
  　　　25 King Creator blanks (KC0000)
- PO No. 1001
  Vendor: Clarke Foam (CLA132)
  Date: 9/30/2006
  Inventory Ordered:
  　　　20 Imposer blanks (IM0000)
  　　　20 Nice Devil blanks (ND0000)
- PO No. 1002
  Vendor: Clarke Foam (CLA132)
  Date: 10/20/2006
  Inventory Ordered:
  　　　15 Imposer blanks (IM0000)
  　　　10 King Creator blanks (KC0000)

The Purchase Order Report

The Purchase Order we have created is an online form and is for internal purposes only. Just as with the Sales Invoice, we need to create a Purchase Order that we can mail to our suppliers. This requires the use of the Report object.

1. Click on the **Reports** object. Double-click on **Create report by using Wizard**.

2. Select **Purchase Order Table** from the **Tables/Queries** pull-down menu. Select all the fields for inclusion by clicking on the $\gg$ button.

NOTE: When performing these next steps, remember to place your cursor on the last field selected prior to selecting fields from the next table to ensure that the fields will be in the correct order in the **Purchase Order Report**.

3. Select the **Supplier Table** and select all fields for inclusion. Return the **SupplierTable.SupplierID** field and the **SupplierPhone** field to the Available Fields window.

4. Select the **PO Inventory Table** and select **InventoryID** and **POQuantityOrdered** fields for inclusion.

5. Select the **Inventory Table** and select the **InventoryDescription** and **InventoryCost** fields for inclusion.

6. Click on **Next**. Accept the layout for the report design presented by the Report Wizard by clicking **Next**.

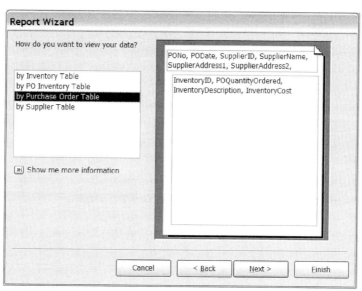

FIGURE 5-15

7. We do not need to add any additional groupings. Click on **Next**. Select **InventoryID** in the sort order combo box and click on **Next**.

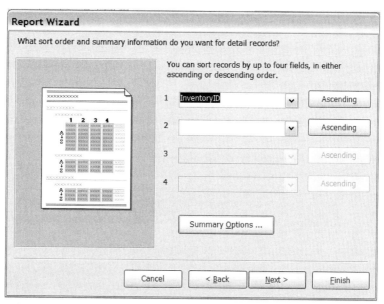

FIGURE 5-16

8. Choose a layout for the report and click on **Next**. (Note that we have chosen Align Left 1 for our layout.) Select a style and click on **Next**. (Note that we have chosen Casual for our report style.)

9. Change the report title to **Purchase Order Report** and click on **Modify the report's design**. Click **Finish**.

10. Drag the top of the Detail section bar down to make room in the PONo Header section. Drag all the fields in the Detail section down to meet the Detail section bar.

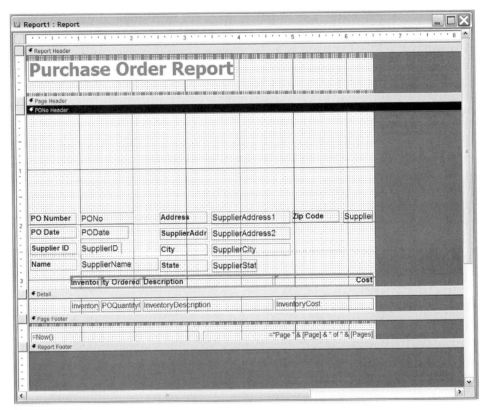

FIGURE 5-17

11. Drag all the fields (including the lines) from the Report Header section to the PONo Header section. Change the label from **Purchase Order Report** to **Purchase Order**.

12. Click on **View** and deselect **Page Header/Footer**. When asked if you want to delete the section and all the controls in them, click **Yes**.

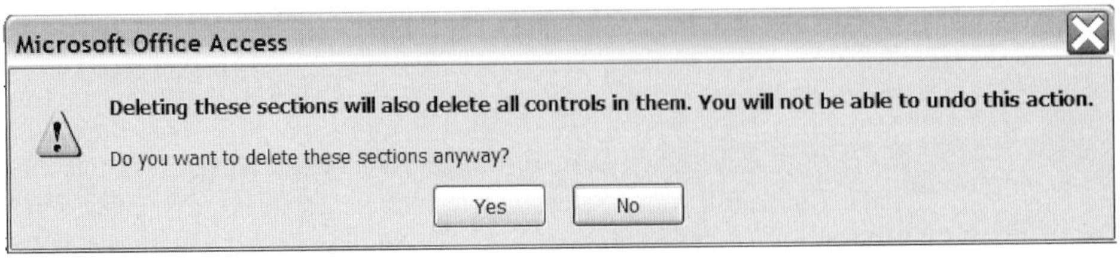

FIGURE 5-18

13. Click on **View** and deselect **Report Header/Footer** in the same manner.

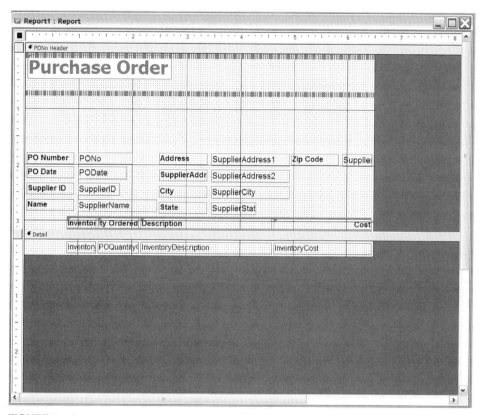

FIGURE 5-19

14. Right-click on the Report Selector (the box between the two rulers) and select Properties or click on **View** > **Properties**. Click on the All tab and click on the Build button for the Record Source to invoke the Query Builder.

15. We want to make a composite address for the supplier, as we did for the customer. Scroll to the right in the design grid until you find an empty field. Place your cursor in the Field property and click on the Build icon. Open the Tables in the lower left side of the Expression window and double-click on the **Supplier Table**. In the upper portion of the Expression Window, type **SupplierCompAddress:**. Double-click on **SupplierCity**; click on **&**; type **", "** (typed as an open quotation, comma, space, close quotation); click on **&**; double-click on **SupplierState**; click on **&**; type **" "** (typed as an open quotation, three spaces, close quotation); click on **&**; and double-click on **SupplierZip**. Remove the ≪**Expr**≫ that was automatically inserted just after the **SupplierCompAddress** field name from the expression. Click **OK**.

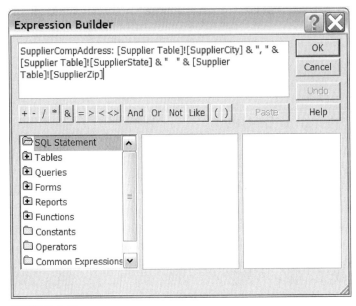

FIGURE 5-20

16. We also want to be able to extend to cost of the inventory ordered. Place your cursor in the next Field property and click on the Build icon. Open the Tables in the lower left side of the Expression window and double-click on the **PO Inventory Table**. Type **Extension:** and double-click on **POQuantityOrdered**. Double-click on *; double-click on the **Inventory Table** and double-click on **InventoryCost**. Remove the ≪**Expr**≫ that was automatically inserted just after the **Extension** field name from the expression (and any other ≪**Expr**≫ that may have appeared in your expression). Click **OK**.

17. Click on the **Run** icon the query. Close and save the query by clicking the X in the upper-right corner. Close the Property window.

18. Delete the **SupplierCity**, **SupplierState**, and **SupplierZip** Text Boxes and Labels from the **Purchase Order Report**.

19. Delete the Labels for the **SupplierAddress1** and **SupplierAddress2** fields and drag the Text Boxes down to make room for the **SupplierName** (see Figure 5-21).

20. Delete the Label for the **SupplierName** field and drag the Text Box above the **SupplierAddress1** field.

21. Click on the **Field List** icon and drag the **SupplierCompAddress** to the PONo Header section, below the **SupplierAddress2** field. Delete the Label.

22. Adjust the field lengths for the address fields.

23. Now we need to look at the remainder of the Detail section. Make sure that all of the data are clearly visible. In the layout we have chosen, for example, many of the labels are truncated and the cost label needs to be realigned so that it is left-justified. We also need to make room for the **Extension** field to the right of the **InventoryCost** field.

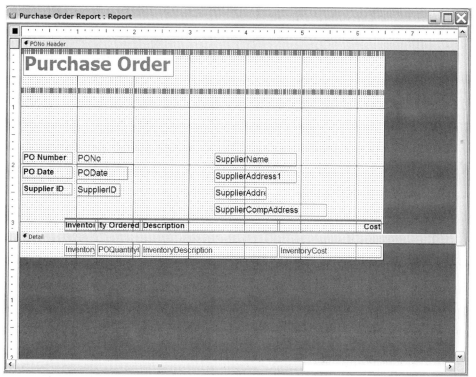

FIGURE 5-21

24. Examine the layout for your report and make the necessary adjustments to make the report more user-friendly and add the **Extension** field. Right-click on the **Extension** field and click on Properties. Change the Format property to Currency. Close the Properties window. Click on the label that was created with the **Extension** field. Change the label to "Extension." Click on **Ctrl-X**, click in the PONo Header section, and then click on **Ctrl-V**. Drag the Extension label to just above the **Extension** field.

25. We also need to add Tragg's name, address, and phone number (provided to you on page 56), identifying the sender of the Purchase Order to the supplier. We do this by clicking on the Label ![icon] icon and typing in the necessary information. Note that you can only use one font size in one Label Box. We typically see the company name larger than the address information. Therefore, to use varying font sizes so that you can make the company name larger than the address information, you will need to make two Label Boxes. When entering the address information, hold down the shift key and hit enter to add a line for the city, state, and zip information, etc.

26. Finally, we need to sum the **Extension** field to arrive at a total for the **Purchase Order Report**. Similar to what we did for the **Sales Invoice Report**, this requires the addition of a PONo Footer. Click on **View** > **Sorting and Grouping**. Change the Group Footer property value to Yes and the Keep Together property value to Whole Group. Close the window.

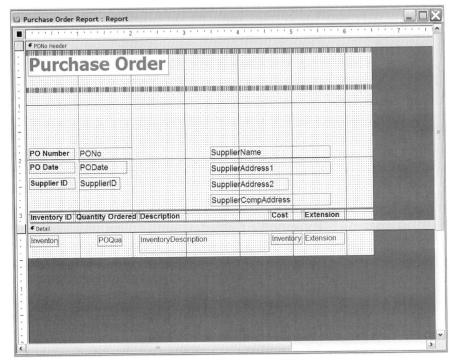

FIGURE 5-22

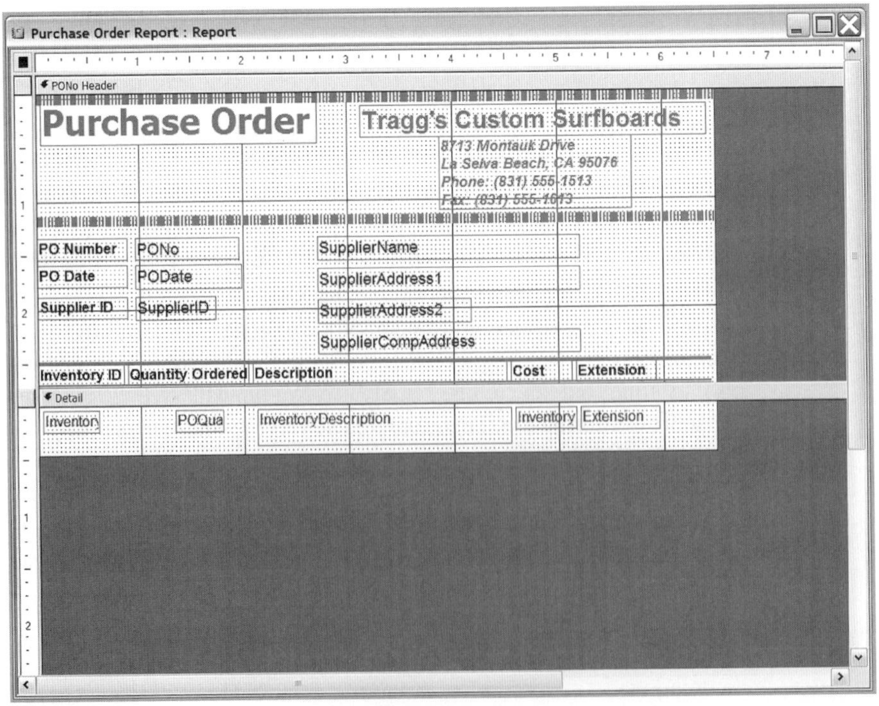

FIGURE 5-23

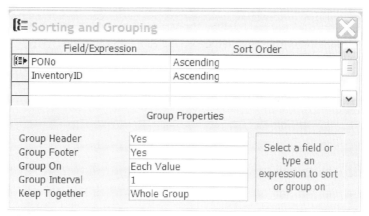

FIGURE 5-24

27. Click on the Text Box ![ab] icon. In the PONo Footer Section, draw a Text Box under the **Extension** field for the **ExtensionTotal** field. Right-click on the Text Box and click on Properties. Under the Control Source property, type = **Sum([Extension])**. Change the caption for the label for the Text Box to **Purchase Order Total**.

28. Right-click on the new Text Box and click on Properties. Click on the Format tab and change the Format property to Currency. Close the window.

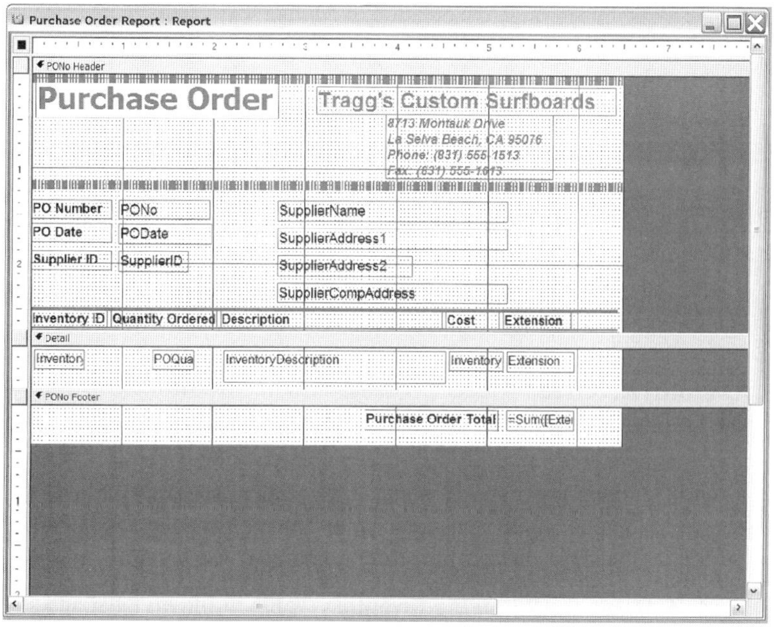

FIGURE 5-25

29. To avoid more than one **Purchase Order** printing on a single page, right-click on the PONo Footer and click on Properties. Under the Format tab, change to Force New Page property to After Section. Close the Properties window.

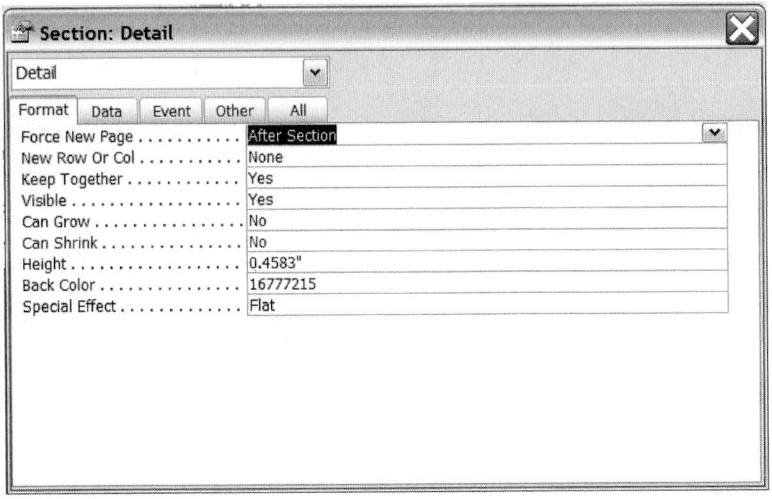

FIGURE 5-26

30. Close and save the **Purchase Order Report**.

The Receiving Report Form

Once the goods are ordered, we need to record their receipt upon delivery to the company. We do this through the creation of another form. Note that, while the Receiving Report is called a "Report," we do not have to create a *Report* in *Access* since this is an internal form.

1. Begin by opening the Relationships ⊞ window. Click on the Show Table ⊞ icon and add the **Receiving Report Table** and the **Receiving Inventory Table** to the Relationships window.

2. Create the required links based on the REA Diagram provided for you in Figure 5-1 and the table structure that followed. Enforce referential integrities where necessary. Close and save your changes to the Relationships window.

3. Click on the **Forms** object and double-click on **Create form by using wizard**. Select the **Receiving Report Table** from the pull-down menu and select all the fields. Select the **Receiving Inventory Table** and select the **InventoryID** and **QuantityReceived** fields. Select the **Inventory Table** and select the **InventoryDescription** field. Click **Next**.

4. Accept the view by Receiving Report Table.

5. Click on Tabular for the layout in the next window and click on **Next**. Choose a style and click on **Next**. Change the title of the form to **Receiving Report Form** and click on **Modify the form's design**. Click on **Finish**.

6. Delete the **Receiving Inventory Table Subform** label and stretch the subform to the left.

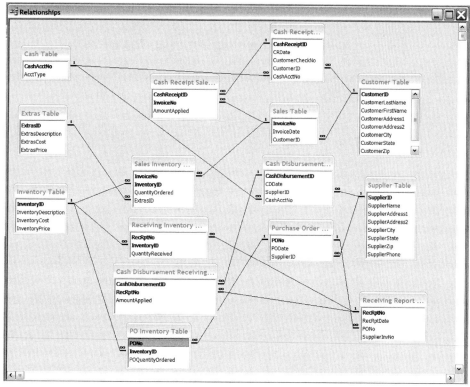

FIGURE 5-27

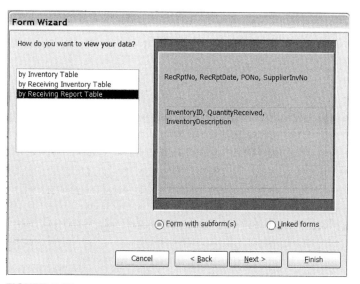

FIGURE 5-28

7. Increase the width of the main form to approximately 6½ inches. Increase the width of the subform to approximately 6¼ inches.

8. It would be beneficial if the users had the Supplier's name on the **Receiving Report Table**. To provide this, we have to have access to the **Supplier Table**. Right-click on the Form Selector (between the two rulers) and select Properties or select **View > Properties**. Click on the Data tab. Click on the **Build** ▦▦ button for the Record Source of the form and invoke the Query Builder.

9. Click on the **Show Table** ▦ icon and add the **Supplier Table**. Notice that there is no relationship between the **Receiving Report Table** and the **Supplier Table**. As a result, we will not be able to add the **SupplierName** to the form. We need to create a link between the two tables first. Think about what table will provide a link between these two tables. The **Purchase Order Table** satisfies this requirement. Add the **Purchase Order Table** and notice that the relationships automatically appear between the three tables.

10. Drag all the fields from the **Receiving Report Table** to the first four fields of the design grids. Drag the **SupplierID** field from the **Purchase Order Table** to the fifth field. Drag the **SupplierName** from the **Supplier Table** to the sixth field.

11. Click on the **Run** ▦ icon. Close and save the query. Close the Properties window.

12. Now that we have created a relationship between the **Receiving Report Table** and the **Supplier Table**, we can add the **SupplierName**. Click on the Field List ▦ icon. Drag the **SupplierName** field to the upper right side of Detail section of the form. Delete the label and stretch out the field to be sure there is enough room for the **SupplierName**.

13. Move the **SupplierInvNo** field below the **SupplierName**.

14. Exchange the positions of the **QuantityReceived** field and the **InventoryDescription** field.

15. Drag the top of the Detail section bar down and create a title for the form (e.g., **Receiving Report Form**).

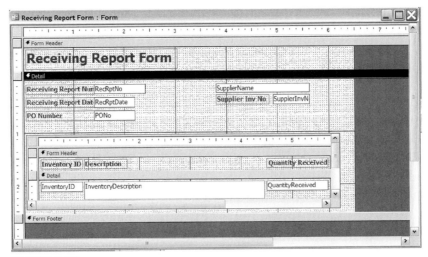

FIGURE 5-29

16. Right-click on **InventoryDescription** and select Properties. Under the Data tab, change the Enable and Locked properties to keep users from changing the description field. Under the Other tab, change the Tab Stop field to No. Under the Format tab, change the Border Style to Transparent. Close the Properties window.

17. Close and save the form.

18. Receive the Purchase Orders created in the previous exercise, as follows:
- PO No. 1000 was received on 9/23/2006 (all items were received)
    - Vendor: SeaFoam (SEA100)
    - Supplier Inv No. 87462
    - Inventory Ordered:
        - 40 Egotists blanks (EG0000)
        - 25 King Creator blanks (KC0000)
- PO No. 1001 was received on 10/6/2006 (all items were received)
    - Vendor: Clarke Foam (CLA132)
    - Supplier Inv No 9475
    - Inventory Ordered:
        - 20 Imposer blanks (IM0000)
        - 20 Nice Devil blanks (ND0000)
- PO No. 1002 was received on 10/28/2006 (all items were received)
    - Vendor: Clarke Foam (CLA132)
    - Supplier Inv No 9589
    - Inventory Ordered:
        - 15 Imposer blanks (IM0000)
        - 10 King Creator blanks (KC0000)

Multistep Queries

We created some simple queries in the Sales/Collection Business Process. However, we can create more complex queries to obtain more detailed information from the database. For example, Dan Tragg keeps close watch on his accounts payable and wishes to obtain the outstanding payable amount at the end of each month. This query requires multiple steps.

1. Click on the **Queries** object. Click on **Create query in Design view**. Click on the **Inventory Table**, hold down the **Ctrl** key, and click on the **Receiving Inventory Table** and the **Receiving Report Table** in the Show Table window, click **Add** and click **Close**.

2. Drag **RecRptDate** into the first column of the design grid. Click on the **Totals** Σ icon. Change the **Total** property for **RecRptDate** to Where and change the Criteria property to $< = $ **[BSDate]**. We are using a wild card because this is a query that Dan Tragg uses every month. The criteria must be "$< = $" so that it includes all purchases up to and including the date that is provided when prompted.

3. Place your cursor in the Field property of the second column in the design grid and click on the Build icon. Double-click on Tables in the lower left portion of the Expression Builder window and click on the **Receiving Inventory Table**. Type **InventoryPurchased:** in the upper portion of the window and double-click on **QuantityReceived** in the middle window in the lower portion of the Expression Builder. Type "*". Click on **Inventory Table** and double-click on **InventoryCost**. Remove the $\ll$**Expr**$\gg$ portion of the expression. Click **OK** to close the Expression Builder window.

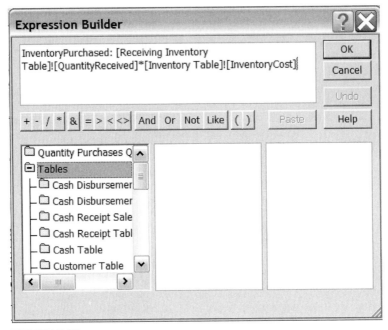

FIGURE 5-30

4. Click on the **Run** [icon] icon to see the results of the query, entering 10/31/2006 when prompted for a date.

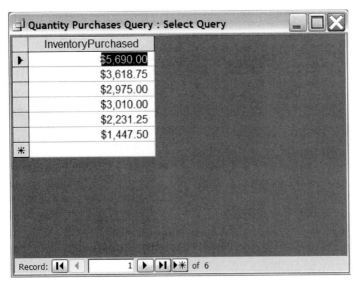

FIGURE 5-31

5. Save the query as **Quantity Purchases Query**.

6. Click on **Create query in Design view** again. We need to sum up the **InventoryPurchased** field we just created. Click on the Queries tab and double-click on the **Quantity Purchases Query** to add it. Close the Show Table window.

7. Drag the **InventoryPurchased** field to the first field in the design grid. Click on the Totals Σ icon. Change the Total property to Sum.

8. Click on the **Run** ▨ icon to see the results of the query, entering 10/31/2006 when prompted for a date.

9. Close and save the query as **Sum Purchases Query**.

10. Click on **Create query in Design view** again. Click on **Cash Disbursement Table**, hold down the **Ctrl** key, and click on the **Cash Disbursement Receiving Table** in the Show Table window, click **Add**, and click **Close**.

11. Drag **AmountApplied** from the **Cash Disbursement Receiving Table** to the first field in the design grid. Drag **CDDate** from the **Cash Disbursement Table** to the second field in the design grid.

12. Click on the Totals Σ icon. Change the Total property for **AmountApplied** to Sum. Change the Total property for **CDDate** to Where. Enter "< = [BSDate]" as the Criteria property for **CDDate**.

13. Click on the **Run** ▨ icon to see the results of the query, again entering 10/31/2006 when prompted for a date.

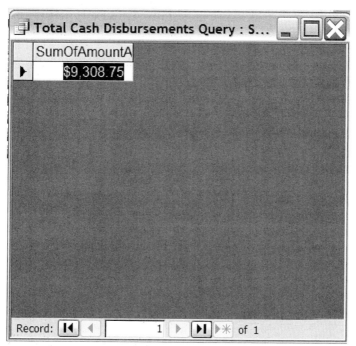

FIGURE 5-32

14. Close and save the query as **Total Cash Disbursements Query**.

15. There is one more step we have to make to arrive at outstanding accounts payable. Click on **Create query in Design view** once more. However, this time we will click on the Queries tab. Notice that we have the two queries that we have just created listed here. Click on the **Total Cash Disbursements Query**, hold down the **Ctrl** key, and click on the **Sum Purchases Query** in the Show Table window, click **Add** and click **Close**.

16. Drag **SumOfInventoryPurchased** into the first field of the design grid and **SumOfAmountApplied** into the second field of the design grid.

17. We need to create a field for the Accounts Payable calculation in the third field. Click on the Field property on the third field and click on the **Build** icon.

18. It is possible (although not likely, unless we were at the beginning of the period) that we could have null values if there were no purchases during the period. *Access* cannot handle null values in a calculation and it returns a null value. To deal with this possibility, we insert the "null-to-zero" or Nz function into every part of the expression in which there is a possibility of a null value. (Note that it must be applied to each part of the expression separately rather than to the overall expression or it will evaluate the entire expression for null values.)

In the lower-left window, double-click on the Queries folder and open the **Sum Purchases Query**. In the upper portion of the window, type "**Accounts Payable: Nz(**". Double-click on **SumOfInventoryPurchased** in the middle lower portion of the window to add it to the upper portion of the window. Double-click on **Total Cash Disbursements Query**. Type "**- Nz(**" Double-click on **SumofAmountApplied** in the middle lower portion of the window to add it to the upper portion of the window. Remove the <<**Expr**>> from the beginning of the expression. Click **OK**.

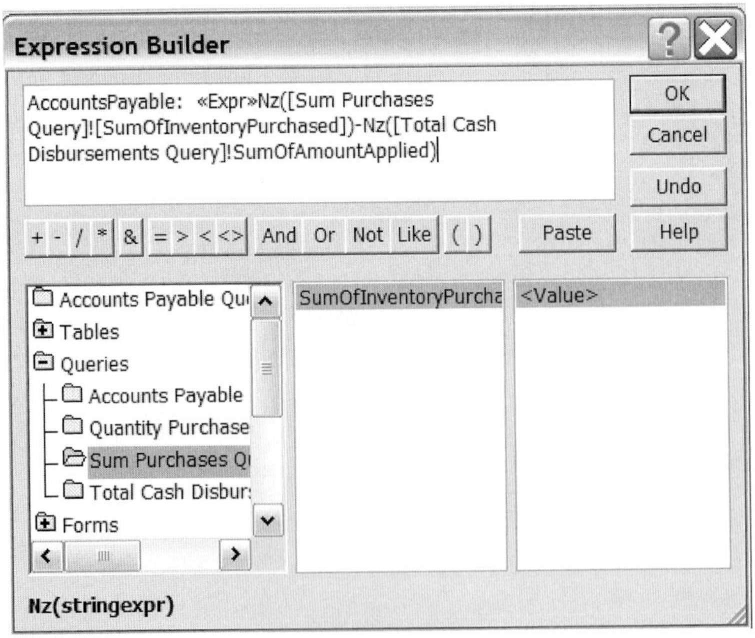

FIGURE 5-33

19. Remove the check mark from the Show property below the **SumOfInventoryPurchased** and **SumOfAmountApplied** fields. We do not need to have them appear in the output when we run the query.

20. Right-click on the **AccountsPayable** field and click on Properties. Change the Format to Currency under the General Tab. Close the Properties window.

FIGURE 5-34

21. Click on the **Run** icon to see the results of the query, again entering 10/31/2006 when prompted for a date.

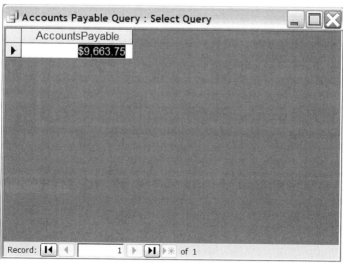

FIGURE 5-35

22. Close and save the query as **Accounts Payable Query**.

KEY TERMS

Acquisition/Payment
business process

Nz (null-to-zero) function

AutoNumber

QUESTIONS AND PROBLEMS FOR REVIEW

MULTIPLE-CHOICE QUESTIONS

5.1 When we convert an REA diagram (a conceptual model) into a relational database,

  (a) We should implement all relationships, regardless of maximum cardinalities, by posting the primary key of one entity into the other entity's table as a foreign key.

  (b) We should implement a 1:1 (one-to-one) relationship with a separate table.

  (c) We should implement a 1:N (one-to-many) relationship by posting the key of the many entity table into the one entity table.

  (d) We should implement a 1:N (one-to-many) relationship by posting the key of the one entity table into the many entity table.

5.2 A company purchases unique (i.e., one-of-a-kind) inventory. The company purchases multiple items from its supplier as part of the same purchase to take advantage of lower shipping costs. The cardinality relationship (based on maximum cardinalities) between purchase and inventory is:

  (a) 1:0

  (b) 1:N

  (c) 1:1

  (d) N:N

  (e) None of the above.

5.3 What is the purpose of the Nz (null-to-zero) function?

  (a) The Nz function enables *Access* to treat null values as if they are zeroes for calculation purposes.

  (b) The Nz function enables *Access* to treat non-null values as if they are null or zero for calculation purposes.

  (c) The Nz function only affects *Access* calculations when there are both non-null and null values.

  (d) The Nz function is only used for complex *Access* calculations.

  (e) None of the above.

PROBLEMS

5.1 Dan Tragg has asked you to calculate the total purchases of each inventory item as of October 31, 2006. Create a query to do this. Your query should include the Inventory ID, quantity, unit cost, and total dollar amount.

5.2 There are many items of inventory listed in the **Inventory Table**. It is hard to keep remembering the item numbers when you are ordering goods. It might make the Purchase Order more user-friendly if we incorporated a pull-down menu for the **Purchase Order Form**. Revise the **Purchase Order Form** to make the **InventoryID** a combo box. In addition, add a total to the Purchase Order Cost column to provide information for internal decision makers.

5.3 Calculate the balance account payable by supplier as of October 31, 2006.

5.4 Create a **Cash Disbursements Form**. The form should include the Cash Disbursement ID, CD Date, Supplier ID, Supplier Name, Cash Account No., Receiving Report No., Amount Applied, and the total of the Amount Applied (with appropriate labels). Once the form has been created, pay PO No. 1001 on October 13, 2006.

5.5 Calculate the cash balance as of October 31, 2006.

CHAPTER 6

HUMAN RESOURCE BUSINESS PROCESS

INTRODUCTION

The Human Resource business process is often referred to as the *payroll transaction cycle*. The Human Resource process however encompasses more than the disbursement of payments to employees for the labor services they provide. It also includes personnel functions, such as hiring, training, and firing employees. The instigation event in the Human Resource process is the labor requisition. The acquisition of labor is the economic increment event, while the payment for the labor is the economic decrement event (i.e., the cash disbursement).

To model the Human Resource business process in a database, we need to be able to create complex calculations. In addition, payroll contains very sensitive information that should not be readily available to most individuals in an organization. Therefore, it should be protected by internal controls that are not necessary in other cycles. After completing this chapter, you should be able to use *Microsoft Access* to:

- Create default values for fields.
- Imbed internal controls into various fields in the table design.
- Create a customized form to meet the special needs that are found in payroll entry.
- Create a simple macro to facilitate form navigation.
- Create a multistep query.
- Create complex calculations in a query.
- Create a union query.

HUMAN RESOURCE PROCESS OVERVIEW

Basic Concepts and Definitions

We once more look back to Figure 1-3 and see that the payroll cycle interfaces with the conversion cycle, the financing cycle, and the financial reporting system. By applying this to our framework of business processes, we can see that labor is acquired by a company through the Human Resource process. The Human Resource process provides labor to the Conversion process for the production of finished goods, which in turn delivers those goods to the Sales/Collection process for sale and subsequent collection of cash. Note that in service organizations, labor may also be provided to the Revenue process (in which case, it is also an economic decrement event). Once the revenue is collected, it is made available to the Financing process and, in turn, is used to pay for the labor acquired by the Human Resource process. For this to happen, the Human Resource process must include at least one economic event that transfers in the labor (i.e., an increment event). This is the acceptance of the labor services. It must also include at least one economic event that transfers out the cash for wages and salaries (i.e., a decrement event). This is the payroll event (i.e., the payment for the labor services). The Human Resource process for all firms is similar regardless of whether the firm is engaged in manufacturing, in service, or in retail.

Tragg's Custom Surfboards

Additional Background   Dan Tragg has gathered a small but dynamic and enthusiastic workforce for his company. Most of the employees have been with him since the company's inception. Dan is the President and Chief Executive Officer of the company. Casey Cameron, Dan's sister, is the company's Managing Director. Sara Tierno is the company's Marketing Director. Paul Kalmann is the Production Supervisor. Miguel Santana is the Controller. They are all full-time, salaried employees. The remaining employees are also full-time but they are paid on an hourly basis. Brenda Chan, Nancy Wood, and John Walker comprise the sales force. David Sinclair, Theresa Chung, and Juan Santiago are the three full-time production employees. Edward Israel is the accounting clerk.

Model the Payroll Cycle Using REA   Tragg's Human Resource process is relatively simple. If the company needs to hire new employees, Casey Cameron, the Managing Director, places an advertisement in the local newspapers. They also rely on referrals from their existing employees. Casey is responsible for interviewing all potential employees. If they have the appropriate qualifications, she then refers them to the appropriate supervisor (i.e., sales candidates to the Marketing Director, production candidates to the Production Supervisor, and accounting candidates to the Controller). She discusses the candidates with the appropriate supervisor and makes the final decision with regard to hiring the individual.

When an employee is hired, the accounting clerk enters his or her personnel information into the database. The sales force, production team, and accounting clerk are paid on an hourly basis. Tragg's pays all employees for holidays and pays the hourly staff time-and-a-half for overtime. All employees are paid on the 15th and the last day of the month.

On payday (the 15th or the last day of the month or the first business day following that day), the supervisor for each department verifies the accuracy of each employee's timecard and inputs the hours for each into the database. One copy of the timecard is filed in the department and another is sent to the accounting department for filing. (It is important to note that this part of the process is not actually part of the payroll process but rather actually part of the conversion process and is, therefore, not described in Figure 5-1.)

The database automatically calculates payroll based upon the information that has been entered into it. The accounting clerk is responsible for verifying the gross pay, withholdings, and net pay dollar amounts that are calculated by the database and for printing the payroll checks.

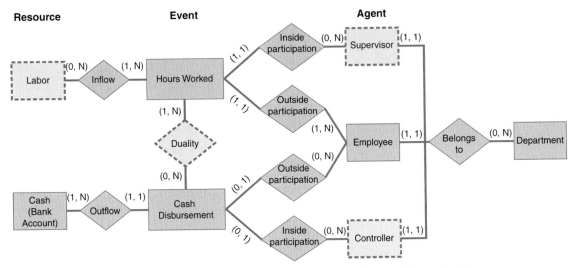

FIGURE 6-1 Basic REA Diagram for Tragg's Custom Surfboards Payroll Cycle

There is a separate checking account for payroll. Payroll checks are approved by the Controller. They are signed by Dan Tragg. This basic process is described in Figure 6-1.

In order to create the payroll, however, there are several other 'entities' involved. For example, it is necessary to reference the number of withholding allowances an individual has claimed and the withholding tables for tax calculation purposes. Therefore, we need to amend Figure 6-1 to include these additional reference tables (see Figure 6-2).

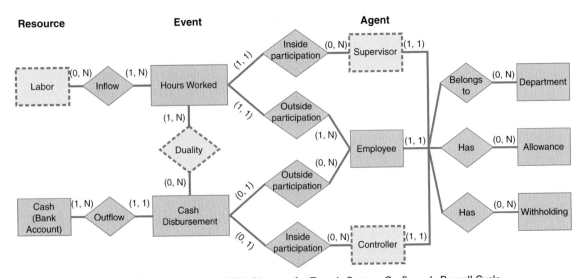

FIGURE 6-2 Amended REA Diagram for Tragg's Custom Surfboards Payroll Cycle

Create a Relational Database for Tragg's Following the REA Diagram

Tragg's table structure for the Human Resource Business Process can be represented as follows:

Cash Table (<u>CashAcctNo</u>, AcctType)

Department Table (<u>DeptNo</u>, DeptDescription)

Hours Worked Table (<u>EmployeeNo</u>, <u>PPEnded</u>, RegularTimeHours, OvertimeHours)

Employee Table (<u>EmployeeNo</u>, EmployeeLastName, EmployeeFirstName,

    EmployeeMiddleInitial, EmployeeSSNo, EmployeeAddress1, EmployeeAddress2, EmployeeCity, EmployeeState, EmployeeZip, EmployeePhone, DateOfBirth, MaritalStatus, <u>TaxBracket</u>, <u>AllowanceNo</u>, PayStatus, HPayRate, SPayRate, EmployeeStartDate, <u>DeptNo</u>, JobTitle)

Withholding Table (<u>TaxBracket</u>, TaxRate, FWT, UpperLimit)

Allowance Table (<u>AllowanceNo</u>, AllowanceAmount)

Notice that we did not include the **Cash Disbursement Table** in our table structure because it has already been created in Chapter 5.

Tragg's Relational Database Using Access   We have created the tables for you in the other chapters. However, the Payroll Cycle contains a great deal of sensitive information. Therefore, there is the opportunity to implement controls and constraints as we build the tables in this cycle. We will start by building the **Employee Table**.

The Employee Table

The **Employee Table** holds data regarding the employee's personal information, the employee's job information, and the employee's payroll information.

1. Click on the **Tables** object and click on **Create table in Design view**.

2. The first field will be the **EmployeeNo**. We will have no need to perform any calculations on this field; therefore, set the Data Type to **Text**. Set the field as the Primary Key. Now move to the Field Properties and set the Field Size to **4**. The Caption should be **Employee No**. It is a required field.

3. The Data Types for the following fields should all be set to Text. The second field is **EmployeeLastName**, the Field Size is 30, and the Caption should be **Last Name**. The third field is **EmployeeFirstName**, the Field Size is 20, and the Caption should be **First Name**.

4. The fourth field is **EmployeeMiddleInitial**, the Field Size is 1, and the Caption should be **Middle Initial**. We will use an Input Mask for this field to assist the users with input of the data. In the Input Mask property, type >**L**. This will ensure than the input is alphabetic and will convert any lower case input into upper case.

5. The fifth field is **EmployeeSSNo**, the Field Size is 11, and the Caption is **Social Security No**. We will again use an Input Mask for this field. However, this time we will use the Build ▦ button next to the Input Mask property. When asked if you want to save the table, click **Yes**. When the Input Mask Wizard window appears, select the Social Security Number option and click **Next**. Click **Next** in the following two windows to accept the input mask and the manner in which it is stored, and then click **Finish**.

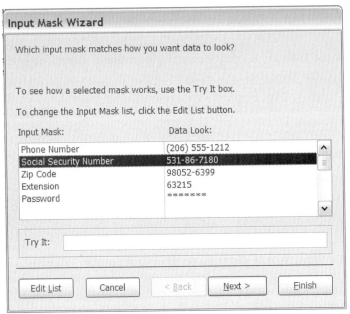

FIGURE 6-3

6. The sixth field is **EmployeeAddress1**, the Field Size is 35, and the Caption is **Address**. The seventh field is **EmployeeAddress2**, the Field Size is 10, and there is no Caption since this is the second line to the Address field. The eighth field is **EmployeeCity**, the Field Size is 25, and the Caption is **City**. The ninth field is **EmployeeState**, the Field Size is 2, and the Caption is **State**. We will again use an Input Mask for this field to assist the users on input of the data. In the Input Mask property, type >**LL**. As we saw with the **EmployeeMiddleInitial** field, this will ensure than the input is alphabetic and will convert any lower case input into upper case.

7. The tenth field is **EmployeeZip**, the Field Size is 10, and the Caption is **Zip Code**. We will again use an Input Mask for this field. However, this time we will use the Build ▦ button next to the Input Mask property to invoke the Input Mask Wizard. Use the Zip Code Input Mask as we did for the **Customer Table** and the **Supplier Table** (in Chapters 4 and 5). Complete the steps in the Input Mask Wizard.

8. The eleventh field is **EmployeePhone**, the Field Size is 14, and the Caption is **Phone Number**. Once again, click on the Build button to invoke the Input Mask Wizard and select the Phone Number Input Mask. Complete the steps in the Input Mask Wizard.

9. The twelfth field is **DateOfBirth**. We will change the Data Type to Date/Time. Once again, click on the Build button to invoke the Input Mask Wizard and select the Short Date Input Mask. Click on **Finish**. The Caption is **Date of Birth**.

10. The thirteenth field is **MaritalStatus**, the Field Size is 1, and the Caption is **Marital Status**. The Data Type is Text. We will use an Input Mask for this field to assist the users on input of the data. In the Input Mask property, type >**L**. Unless an employee declares his or her marital status to be married, by default the law considers them to be single. Therefore, we will set the Default Value at "**S**." We also want to ensure that no value other than "**M**" for Married or "**S**" for Single is entered in this field. Thus, we will set the Validation Rule as = **"S" Or "M"**. Finally, we want to include a Validation Text informing the user of the input requirements should he or she make an invalid entry in this field. Type "**Enter S for Single; M for Married**" in the Validation Text property.

11. The fourteenth field is **TaxBracket**, the Data Type is Text, the Field Size is 2, and the Caption is **Tax Bracket**.

12. The fifteenth field is **AllowanceNo** and the Data Type is Number. The Field Size is Byte and the Decimal Places is set to 0 since the value for this field will always be a whole number. The Caption is **Allowance No**.

13. The sixteenth field is **PayStatus**, the Data Type is Text, the Field Size is 1, and the Caption is **Pay Status**. The Data Type is Text. Use the Input Mask property to assist the users on input of the data by typing >**L**. We want to ensure that no value other than "**H**" for Hourly or "**S**" for Salaried is entered in this field. Thus, we will set the Validation Rule as = **"H" Or "S"**. We also want to include a Validation Text informing the user of the input requirements should he or she make an invalid entry in this field. Type "**Enter H for Hourly; S for Salaried**" in the Validation Text property.

14. The seventeenth field is **HPayRate**, the Data Type is Currency, and the Format is Currency. Set the Decimal Places to 2 and the Caption to **Hourly Pay Rate**.

15. The eighteenth field is **SPayRate**, the Data Type is Currency, and the Format is Currency. Set the Decimal Places to 2 and the Caption to **Salaried Pay Rate**.

16. The nineteenth field is **EmployeeStartDate**. We will change the Data Type to Date/Time. Once again, click on the Build button to invoke the Input Mask Wizard and select the Short Date Input Mask. Click on **Finish**. The Caption is **Start Date**.

17. The twentieth field is **DeptNo**, the Data Type is Text, the Field Size is 2, and the Caption is **Dept No**.

18. The last field is **JobTitle**, the Data Type is Text, the Field Size is 35, and the Caption is **Job Title**.

The Employee Form

Recall that we created fields in the **Employee Table** for three categories: the employee's personal information, the employee's job information, and the employee's payroll information. As we design the **Employee Form**, we will keep those fields together in separate categories to make the form more user-friendly and to facilitate the input of data.

1. Click on the **Forms** object and click on **New** icon in theTraggsCh6Student: Database menu window. Select Design View and select **Employee Table** from the pull-down menu.

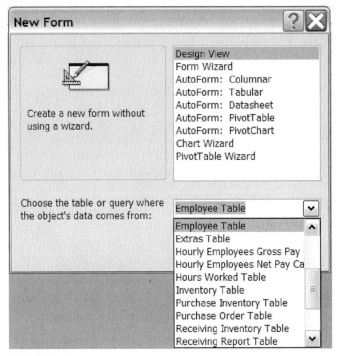

FIGURE 6-4

    2. Click **OK**. Notice that we now have a blank form and the Field List window automatically appears.

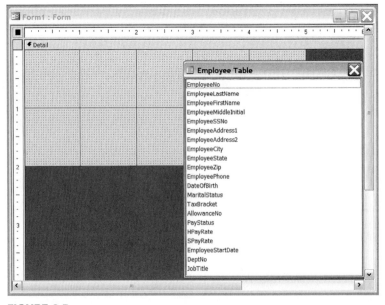

FIGURE 6-5

3. Stretch the form out to the right to approximately 6¼ inches and drag the bottom of the form down to approximately 4½ inches.

4. Click on the **Rectangle** ▦ icon in the Toolbox and, starting in the upper left-hand corner of the form, drag a rectangle out approximately 2½ inches wide and 3¼ inches long.

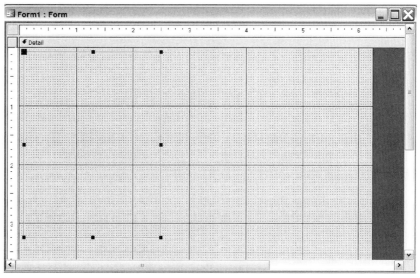

FIGURE 6-6

5. Click on the **Label** ▤ icon in the Toolbox and draw a narrow rectangle for a label centered at the top of the rectangle you just created. Type "**Employee Personal Information**" in this label. Click your cursor outside of this rectangle. Then click the new label once to highlight it. Click on the **Bold** **B** icon and then click on the **Center** ☰ Align icon.

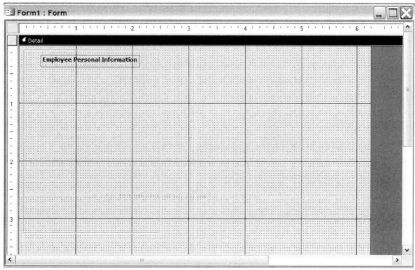

FIGURE 6-7

6. Click on the **Rectangle** ▆ icon again. Draw another rectangle beginning at approximately the 3-inch mark to approximately the 5¾-inch mark on the top ruler and down approximately 1½ inches. Draw another rectangle below that rectangle beginning at approximately the 2¾-inch mark to the 6-inch mark on the top ruler and down to the 3½-inch mark. Click on the **Label** 🔤 icon and draw a label at the center top of the newly created rectangle. Type "**Employee Job Information**" in this label. Center it and make it bold as you did with the label in the first rectangle (see step 5). Make a label for the second new rectangle. Type "**Employee Payroll Information**" in this label, center it, and make it bold.

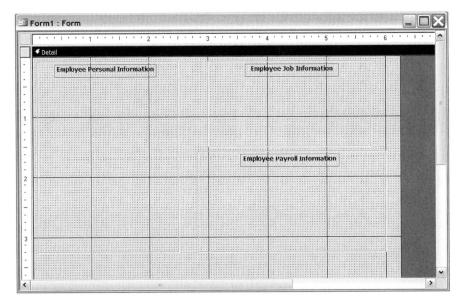

FIGURE 6-8

7. Now we will begin to drag the fields into the three categories we have created. Drag the following fields into the Employee Personal Information rectangle: **EmployeeNo, EmployeeFirstName, EmployeeMiddleInitial, EmployeeLastName, EmployeeAddress1, EmployeeAddress2,** and **EmployeeCity.** Since **EmployeeState** and **EmployeeZip** are not long fields, we can place them next to each other. Drag them into the rectangle and place them next to each other. Drag **EmployeePhone** and **DataOfBirth** into the rectangle. Now that we have the fields that we want in this area, we need to clean this up and make it user-friendly.

8. Stretch the **EmployeeNo** label to the left edge of the rectangle. Click on the label again and drag the right side of the label rectangle so that the right edge of the rectangle meets the left edge of the Text Box. Double-click on the label and delete the colon at the end of the label. Drag the right side of the Text Box to the left to shrink the size of the field.

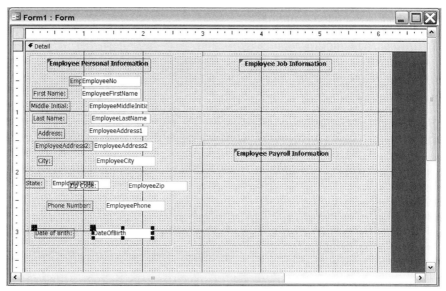

FIGURE 6-9

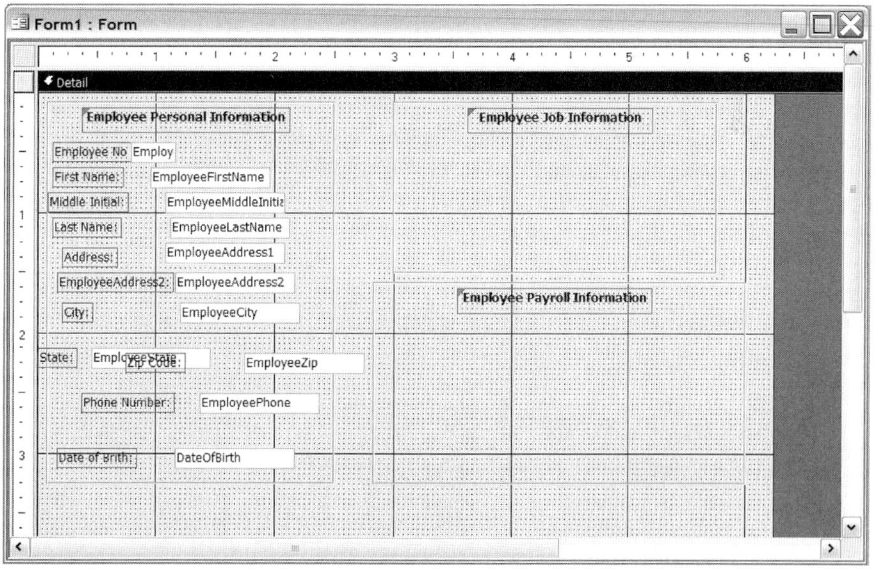

FIGURE 6-10

9. Align the label for **EmployeeFirstName** below the label for **EmployeeNo** but begin the Text Box at approximately the 1-inch mark on the top ruler. Delete the colon from the label and stretch the label out to just beyond the 2-inch mark. Do the same thing for **EmployeeMiddleInitial**, **EmployeeLastName**, **EmployeeAddress1**, **EmployeeAddress2**, and **EmployeeCity**. Delete the label for **EmployeeAddress2**.

10. Align the label for **EmployeeState** below the other labels and shrink the Text Box. Remember that this field only needs to be large enough to accommodate two capital letters. Delete the colon in the label.

11. Move the **EmployeeZip** label and field next to the **EmployeeState** field. Adjust the length of the label and Text Box and delete the colon in the label.

12. Align the label for **PhoneNumber** below the other labels. Delete the colon from the label and stretch the Text Box out to just beyond the 2-inch mark.

13. Leave a small space before going on to the **DateOfBirth** field. Align the label for **DateOfBirth** below the other labels. Delete the colon from the label and stretch the Text Box out to accommodate the date.

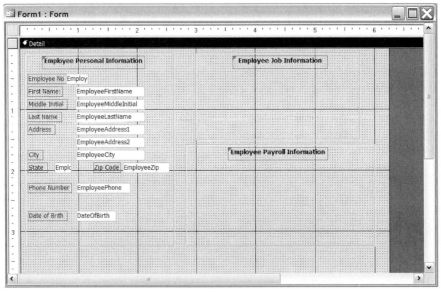

FIGURE 6-11

14. Tragg's does not have very many departments and it would not be very difficult for the accounting clerk to memorize the department numbers. However, it would make the form much more user-friendly and result in fewer input errors if the clerk can select the department name from a pull-down menu. Therefore, we will create a Combo Box for the **DeptNo** field. Click on the **Combo Box** icon and draw a rectangle below the heading label in the Employee Job Information rectangle.

15. When the Combo Box Wizard asks how you want the combo box to get its values, accept the default (i.e., you want to look up the values in a table or query because we will be getting the values from the **DeptNo** field). Click **Next**.

16. Choose the **Department Table** in the next screen and click **Next**.

17. Click the >> to select both fields for inclusion.

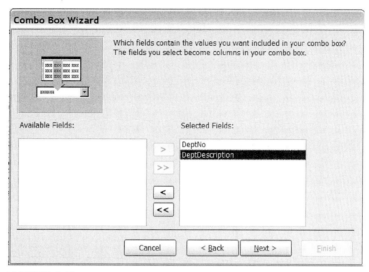

FIGURE 6-12

18. Select **DeptDescription** for the sort order in the next window. Click **Next**.

19. Double-click on the right edge of the column heading to automatically adjust the width of the column. Click **Next**.

20. Click on **Store that value in this field**. Select **DeptNo** from the pull-down menu. This stores the data in the **DeptNo** field. Click **Next**.

21. Enter **Department** as the label for the Combo Box. Click **Finish**.

22. Drag **JobTitle** and **EmployeeStartDate** into the Employee Job Information rectangle. Align the labels for **JobTitle** and **EmployeeStartDate** below the **DeptNo** label. Delete the colon from the labels and stretch the Text Boxes out to accommodate the data.

23. Drag the **EmployeeSSNo**, **MaritalStatus**, and **PayStatus** fields from the Field List into the Employee Payroll Information rectangle. Align the label and Text Box for **MaritalStatus** below the **EmployeeSSNo** label and Text Box. Since the **MaritalStatus** field only contains one character, you can shrink the size of the Text Box. Drag the **PayStatus** label and Text Box next to the **MaritalStatus** field. Again, since the **PayStatus** field only contains one character, you can also shrink the size of this Text Box. Delete the colon from the labels.

24. Drag the **AllowanceNo** and **HPayRate** and **SPayRate** from the Field List into the Employee Payroll Information rectangle. Align the label and Text Box for **AllowanceNo** below the **MaritalStatus** label and Text Box. Align the label and Text Box for **HPayRate** below the **PayStatus** label and Text Box. Then align the label and the Text Box for **SPayRate** below the **HPayRate** label and Text Box. Delete the colon from the labels.

25. The **TaxBracket** field represents another area where we can make good use of the Combo Box. Take a moment and open the **Withholding Table**. Note that the primary key in this table is **TaxBracket**. Therefore, it is a foreign key in the **Employee Table** (just as the **DeptNo** was). We want to be able to determine the appropriate tax bracket for the employee, based upon his or her marital status and pay rate. We can do this by referring to the **Withholding Table**. This table follows the 2005 IRS Tables for Percentage Method of

Withholding. We will explain the calculation to determine federal withholding in more detail later when we create the query to calculate net pay. However, it is important to acquaint yourself now with the structure of the table. The table lists the schedule for married taxpayers first and then lists the schedule for single taxpayers. The second field, **TaxRate**, provides the tax rate to be applied on wages that do not exceed the bracketed amount. The last field, **UpperLimit**, provides the upper limit for the bracket. **FWT** is the amount to be added to the calculated tax to arrive at the total withholding.

The **UpperLimit** field is important to us here because it will help us to determine the **TaxBracket** to choose for each employee. By examining the table, we know that we can look at the **PayRate**, **MaritalStatus**, and **UpperLimit** field and determine the **TaxBracket**. For example, if an employee is married and their **PayRate** is $3,750, his or her **TaxBracket** would be **M3**. It is important to note that, for purposes of simplification and illustration in this text, we have eliminated any possibility that an individual's allowances will reduce their wages to a lower **TaxBracket**. In reality, this tax calculation would involve far more steps than we include in this book. Our purpose is to provide you with a sense of the complexity involved in building the tables, forms, and queries in this cycle. Close the **Withholding Table** now.

26. Click on the **Combo Box** icon and drag a rectangle below the **AllowanceNo** and pay rate fields (both **SPayRate** and **HPayRate**). We want to look the values up in the **Withholding Table**; therefore, click **Next**.

27. Select the **Withholding Table** from the pull-down menu and click **Next**.

28. Select **TaxBracket** and **UpperLimit** from the Available Fields window for inclusion. Click **Next**.

29. Select the **TaxBracket** field for the sort order and click **Next**.

30. Deselect the recommendation to hide the primary key column. We want to have the **TaxBracket** appear on the form. Click **Next**.

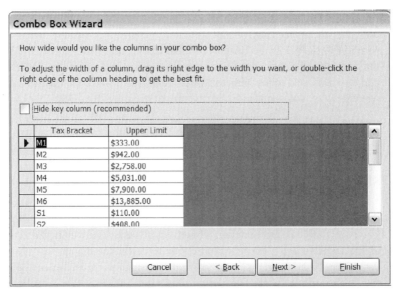

FIGURE 6-13

31. Select **TaxBracket** to store or use in the database and click **Next**.

32. Select **Store that value in this field** and choose **TaxBracket** from the pull-down menu. Click **Next**.

33. Type **Tax Bracket** in the label and click **Finish**.

34. Click on the label for the newly created Combo Box to highlight it. Now hit **Ctrl X**, then **Ctrl V**. The label is now in the upper left-hand corner of the Detail section of the form. Drag it down to the Combo Box and place it above the upper left-hand portion of the Combo Box. This is where the **TaxBracket** field will appear. Click on the Label 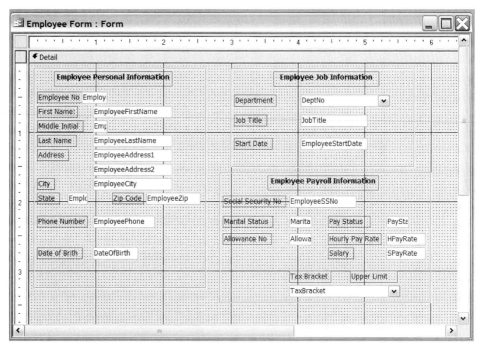 icon and drag a rectangle above the remainder of the Combo Box. Type **Upper Limit** in this label.

FIGURE 6-14

35. We now want to make it easier for users to navigate to the next record. We will create a button to do this. Click on the **Command** button in your Toolbox and draw a rectangle below and outside the lower right-hand corner of the Employee Payroll Information rectangle.

36. Select **Record Navigation** in the Categories window and **Go To Next Record**. Click **Next**.

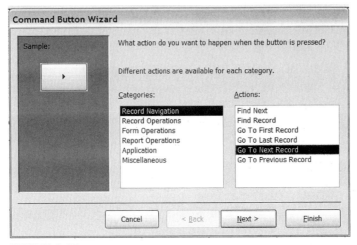

FIGURE 6-15

37. Select **Right Arrow (Black)**. Click **Next**.

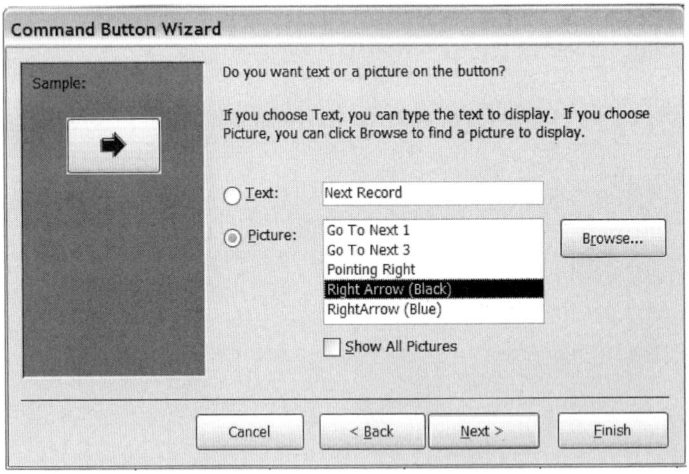

Command Button Wizard

Sample:

Do you want text or a picture on the button?

If you choose Text, you can type the text to display. If you choose Picture, you can click Browse to find a picture to display.

○ Text: Next Record

◉ Picture: Go To Next 1
            Go To Next 3
            Pointing Right
            Right Arrow (Black)
            RightArrow (Blue)

            Browse...

☐ Show All Pictures

Cancel   < Back   Next >   Finish

FIGURE 6-16

38. Type **NextRecord** in the name for the button. Click **Finish**.

39. This button will take us to the next record but we also want to be sure that when the record appears the cursor is in the first field (i.e., in the **EmployeeNo** field). To do this, we will write a short **Macro**. Recall from Chapter 3 that a Macro is an action that we can use to automate a series of steps or tasks. Minimize the **Employee Form**.

40. Click on the **Macros** object and click on **New** .

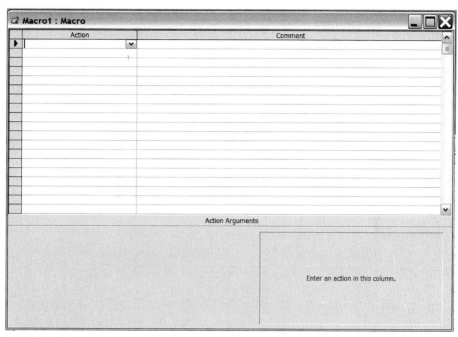

FIGURE 6-17

41. Note that the design window for the Macro has two columns. The first column is for the Action. An Action is the foundation of a **Macro**. The Action is the instruction; it can be combined with other Actions to automate tasks. The second column is a Comment field, similar to the Description field in the **Tables** object.

42. Type **Echo** in the first Action field and "**Hide the results of the macro while it runs**" in the Comment field. This has the effect of hiding the macro so the user is unaware of its movements.

43. Type **GoToRecord** in the second Action field and "**Move to the next record**" in the second Comment field. This has the effect of taking the user to the next record. Notice that the lower portion of the window changes at this point. The Action Arguments default makes the specified record the Next record.

44. Type **GoToControl** in the third Action field and "**Move the focus to the first field, Employee No**" in the Comment field. Type **EmployeeNo** in the Control Name field in the Action Arguments portion of the window. This tells the Macro where to go when it moves to the next record.

45. Close and save the Macro as **Next Record**.

46. Restore the **Employee Form** that you minimized. Right-click on the Command button and click on Properties. Click on the Event tab. Pull-down the menu next to the On Click property and change the selection to the newly created macro, **Next Record**.

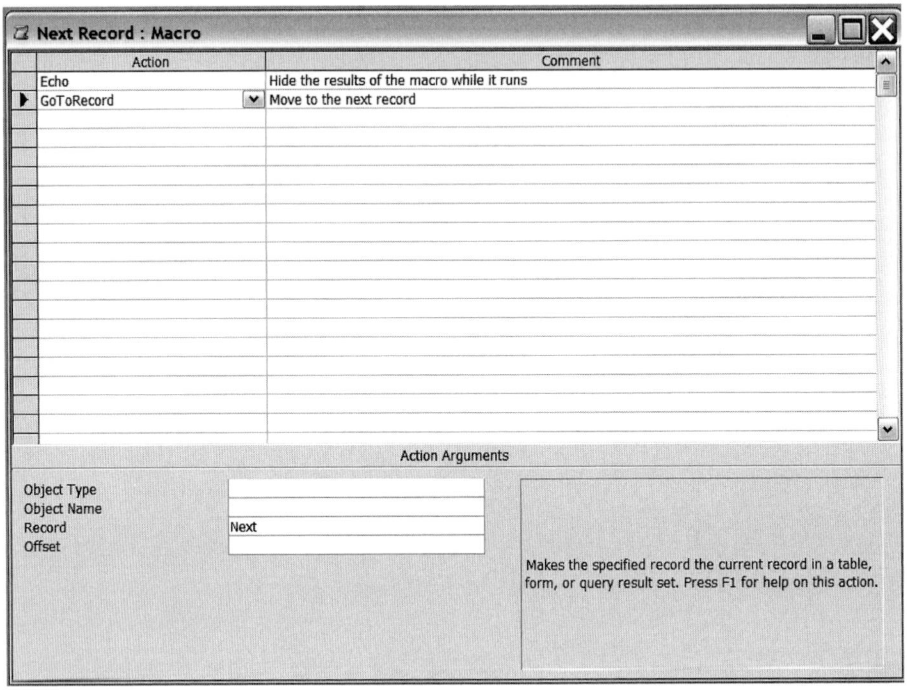

FIGURE 6-18

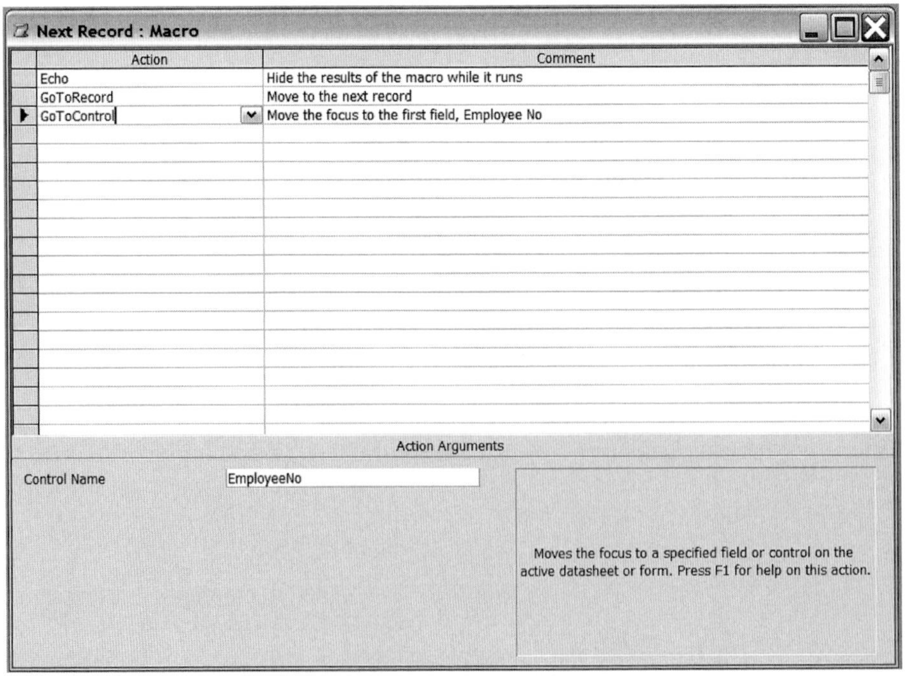

FIGURE 6-19

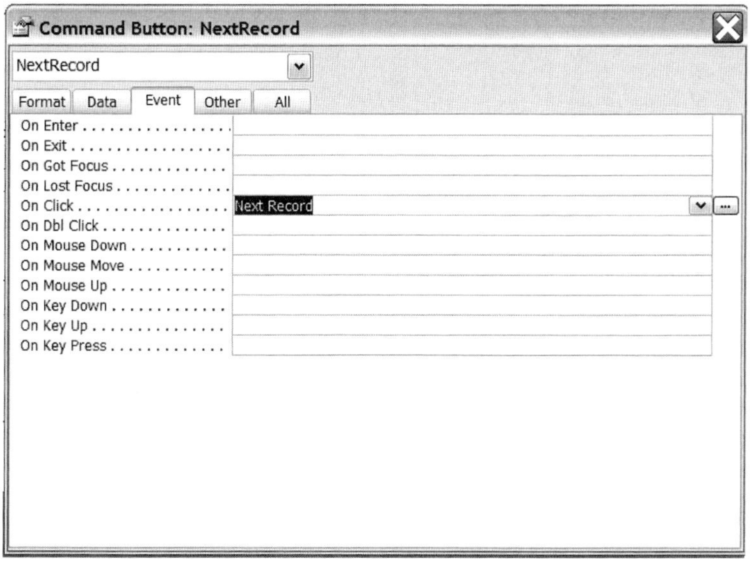

FIGURE 6-20

47. Close the Properties window.

48. Close and save the form as **Employee Form**.

49. Enter the following employee data at this time. We realize that this data entry is a tedious job. However, the data is necessary for the remainder of your practice to learn about the payroll process.

- Employee No 1001
  Dan W Tragg
  8713 Montauk Place
  La Selva Beach, CA 96076
  (831) 555-4374
  DOB 12/30/1967
  Dept: Administration
  Job Title: President
  Start Date: 9/1/1988
  SSN: 630-30-3003
  Marital Status: M
  Pay Status: S
  Allowances: 2
  Pay Rate: $5,500.00
  Tax Bracket: M4
- Employee No 1002
  Casey C Cameron
  12773 Calma Court
  La Selva Beach, CA 96076
  (831) 555-4373

DOB 12/3/1970
Dept: Administration
Job Title: Managing Director
Start Date: 9/1/1988
SSN: 630-30-3113
Marital Status: S
Pay Status: S
Allowances: 0
Pay Rate: $4,000.00
Tax Bracket: S4

- Employee No 1003
Sara K Tierno
8713 Montauk Place
La Selva Beach, CA 96076
(831) 555-4374
DOB 8/15/1968
Dept: Marketing and Sales
Job Title: Marketing Director
Start Date: 10/19/1990
SSN: 661-77-2937
Marital Status: M
Pay Status: S
Allowances: 1
Pay Rate: $3,500.00
Tax Bracket: M3

- Employee No 1004
Nancy C Wood
22 Greenhill Lane
Santa Cruz, CA 95062
(831) 555-8485
DOB 7/19/1966
Dept: Marketing and Sales
Job Title: Sales
Start Date: 3/16/1999
SSN: 301-55-1918
Marital Status: S
Pay Status: H
Allowances: 0
Pay Rate: $17.25
Tax Bracket: S3

- Employee No 1005
Juan X Santiago
6746 Mission Blvd
Santa Cruz, CA 95062
(831) 555-7864
DOB 6/17/1960

Dept: Production
Job Title: Production
Start Date: 5/23/2001
SSN: 600-55-5533
Marital Status: S
Pay Status: H
Allowances: 2
Pay Rate: $17.00
Tax Bracket: S3

- Employee No 1006
Paul Kalmann
2771 Dos Perros Drive
Ben Lomand, CA 94583
(831) 555-7488
DOB 12/10/1973
Dept: Production
Job Title: Production Supervisor
Start Date: 7/13/2001
SSN: 734-79-6289
Marital Status: S
Pay Status: S
Allowances: 0
Pay Rate: $3,250.00
Tax Bracket: S4

- Employee No 1007
David M Sinclair
7364 Labrador Lane
Scotts Valley, CA 95067
(831) 555-9764
DOB 11/21/1982
Dept: Production
Job Title: Production
Start Date: 3/16/2000
SSN: 601-74-5936
Marital Status: S
Pay Status: H
Allowances: 0
Pay Rate: $16.75
Tax Bracket: S3

- Employee No 1008
Theresa S Chung
3819 Lazy Lanc
Santa Cruz, CA 95062
(831) 555-7469
DOB 5/1/1981
Dept: Production

Job Title: Production
Start Date: 6/25/2000
SSN: 587-85-8474
Marital Status: S
Pay Status: H
Allowances: 0
Pay Rate: $16.75
Tax Bracket: S3

- Employee No 1009
Miguel C Santana
7227 Via de la Siesta
Santa Cruz, CA 95062
(831) 555-0847
DOB 8/31/1970
Dept: Accounting
Job Title: Controller
Start Date: 3/27/2002
SSN: 630-30-3113
Marital Status: M
Pay Status: S
Allowances: 1
Pay Rate: $3,250.00
Tax Bracket: M3

- Employee No 1010
John T. Walker
928 Enterprise Drive
Apt. 2A
Santa Cruz, CA 95062
(831) 555-9442
DOB 12/13/1980
Dept: Marketing and Sales
Job Title: Sales
Start Date: 4/14/2002
SSN: 643-67-5837
Marital Status: S
Pay Status: H
Allowances: 0
Pay Rate: $16.50
Tax Bracket: S3

- Employee No 1011
Edward E Israel
9766 Labrador Lane
Scotts Valley, CA 95067
(831) 555-9536
DOB 3/16/1984
Dept: Accounting
Job Title: Accounting clerk

Start Date: 12/28/2003
SSN: 501-38-9574
Marital Status: S
Pay Status: H
Allowances: 0
Pay Rate: $16.50
Tax Bracket: S3
- Employee No 1012
Brenda T Chan
9462 Monterey Lane
Scotts Valley, CA 95067
(831) 555-7316
DOB 2/9/1971
Dept: Marketing and Sales
Job Title: Sales
Start Date: 10/13/2003
SSN: 845-63-6956
Marital Status: S
Pay Status: H
Allowances: 0
Pay Rate: $16.50
Tax Bracket: S3

Tracking Time Worked

In order to calculate payroll, it is necessary to track the hours worked for hourly employees. The **Hours Worked Table** and **Hours Worked Form** have been created for this purpose. Since we have some employees who are production employees and some who are nonproduction employees, this table and form can be considered part of the Conversion Process. Therefore, we have not detailed the construction of these objects in this chapter. Some points are worth noting, however.

Now that we have created the **Employee Table** and **Employee Form**, we can populate the **Hours Worked Table**. Note that we only need to input data for hourly employees into this form. Open the **Hours Worked Form** and input the following data for the pay period ended 9/30/2006:

- Employee No 1004
88 hours Regular Time
1.2 hours Overtime
- Employee No 1005
88 hours Regular Time
2.7 hours Overtime
- Employee No 1007
88 hours Regular Time
0.3 hours Overtime
- Employee No 1008
88 hours Regular Time
0 hours Overtime

- Employee No 1010
  88 hours Regular Time
  0.1 hours Overtime
- Employee No 1011
  88 hours Regular Time
  0 hours Overtime
- Employee No 1012
  88 hours Regular Time
  0.4 hours Overtime

The Gross Pay Query

Since the database has now been populated with employee, payroll, and hours worked data, we can now calculate the payroll. Arriving at net pay is a complex, multistep process and requires the use of queries. We begin with the calculation of gross pay. The calculation for salaried employees and hourly employees is slightly different. Therefore, we need to perform two different queries for gross pay and then merge the two queries together. To do this, we need to be sure that the two queries have matching fields and the same number of columns.

1. Click on the **Queries** object and double-click on **Create query in Design view**.

2. Click on the **Employee Table**, hold the **Ctrl** key down, and click on the **Hours Worked Table**. Click **Add** and then click **Close**.

3. Drag the **EmployeeNo** field from the **Hours Worked Table** into the first column of the design grid. Drag the **PPEnded**, **RegularTimeHours**, and **OvertimeHours** from the **Hours Worked Table** into the next columns of the design grid. Drag **HPayRate** from the **Employee Table** to the next column.

4. Click on the Field property in the sixth column of the design grid and click on the Build icon in the menu bar. Type **HRegularPay: [HPayRate]*[RegularTimeHours]** in the upper portion of the Expression Builder window. Click **OK**.

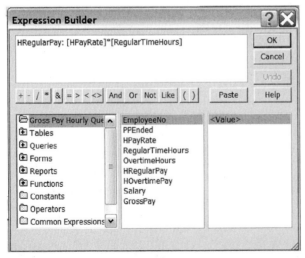

FIGURE 6-21

5. Click on the Field property in the seventh column of the design grid and click on the Build 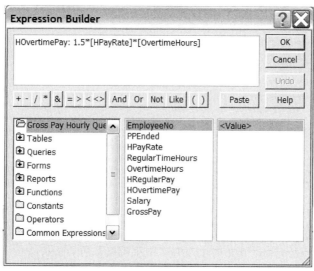 icon in the menu bar. Type **HOvertimePay: 1.5* [HPayRate]* [OvertimeHours]** in the upper portion of the Expression Builder window. Click **OK**.

FIGURE 6-22

6. Before we can calculate the gross pay field, we need to create a field that will hold the place for the gross pay for salaried employees. Click on the Field property in the eighth column of the design grid. Type **Salary: 0** in the Field property. This results in creating a column with the field name "Salary" that is a place holder in this query so that we can join the salaried gross pay data later.

7. Click on the Field property in the ninth column of the design grid and click on the Build 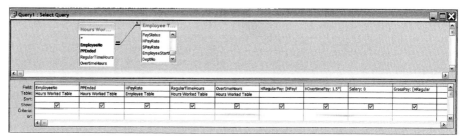 icon in the menu bar. Type **GrossPay: [HRegularPay] + [HOvertimePay] + [Salary]** in the upper portion of the Expression Builder window. Click **OK**.

FIGURE 6-23

8. Click on the Run ![run icon] icon. Close and save the query as **Gross Pay Hourly Query**.

9. Now we will create a query for the salaried employees. Click on **Create query in Design view**. Click on **Employee Table**. This is the only table we will need for salaried employees. Click on **Add** and **Close**.

10. Remember that we must eventually join this query with the query we just created for the hourly employees and, therefore, we must match the columns we created for this query. Open the **Gross Pay Hourly Query** and count the number of columns in that query. We see that, in addition to **EmployeeNo**, we had six fields that related to hourly employees. We then entered a field as a place holder for salaried employees. Finally, we calculated gross pay. Close the **Gross Pay Hourly Query**.

11. We know that we will want **EmployeeNo** in the first field for the salaried employees query. Drag that field from the **Employee Table** first field in the design grid.

12. In the next six Field properties, type a **0**. These columns will now act as place holders, just as the Salary column did in the **Gross Pay Hourly Query**.

13. Drag the **SPayRate** field from the **Employee Table** into the eighth column of the design grid. Click on the Criteria property and type >0. This will result in listing only those employees whose **SPayRate** is greater than zero or, in other words, only salaried employees.

14. Click on the Field property in the ninth column of the design grid and click on the Build 📐 icon in the menu bar. Type **GrossPay: [SPayRate]*1** in the upper portion of the Expression Builder window. Click **OK**.

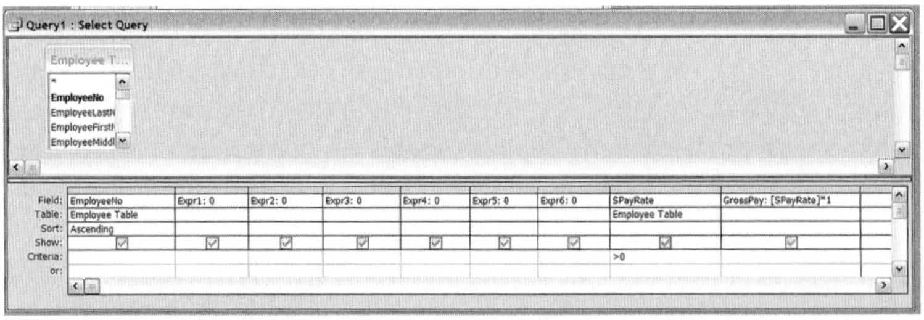

FIGURE 6-24

15. Click on the Run ❗ icon. Close and save the query as **Gross Pay Salaried Query**.

16. We now have to join the two queries together. We will do this by creating a union query. A union query is a type of select query that combines fields from two or more tables or queries into one field in the query's results with any duplicate records removed. Double-click on **Create query in Design view**. Close the **Show Table** window.

17. Click on **Query** in the Menu bar. Click on **SQL Specific > Union**.

18. In the design screen for the union query, type the following SQL statement:

    Select * from [Gross Pay Hourly Query]

    UNION Select * from [Gross Pay Salaried Query];

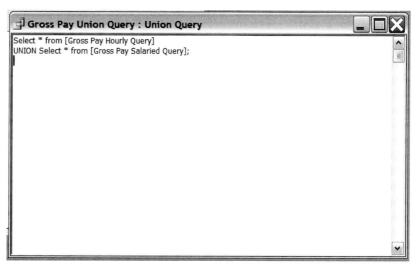

FIGURE 6-25

FIGURE 6-26

19. Close and save the union query as **Gross Pay Union Query**.

We are now ready to calculate net pay. There are many deductions that can go into the calculation of net pay. We will simplify the calculation by limiting the deductions to payroll taxes, specifically federal withholding tax (which we will abbreviate as FIT), FICA (Federal Insurance Corporation Act Tax for Social Security), and Medicare tax. We will ignore state withholding and other deductions such as medical insurance, retirement, etc.

20. Double-click on **Create query in Design view**. Click on the Queries tab in the **Show Table** window and click on the **Gross Pay Union Query**. Click **Add**. Click on the Tables tab. Click on the **Employee Table**, the **Withholding Table**, and the **Allowance Table**. Click **Close**.

21. Drag the **EmployeeNo** from the **Gross Pay Union Query** into the first Field property. Click on the Sort property and click on Ascending.

22. Drag **PPEnded** and **GrossPay** from **Gross Pay Union Query** into the second and third Field properties.

23. Drag **TaxRate**, **FWT**, and **UpperLimit** from **Withholding Table** into the fourth, fifth, and sixth Field properties.

24. Drag **AllowanceAmount** from **Allowance Table** into the seventh Field property.

The following steps relate to the calculation of payroll taxes. These calculations are relatively complex but they serve two important purposes. First, we have not yet learned about complex calculations in a database and they will allow us to practice them. Second, taxation is an important part of the study of accounting. The study of accounting information systems (AIS) requires a solid understanding of the different aspects of accounting. It is important to keep in mind that "accounting" is the first word in AIS!!

25. Click on the Field property in the eighth column of the design grid and click on the Build 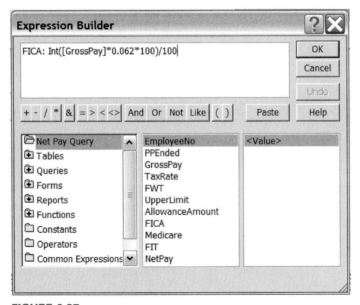 icon in the menu bar. Type **FICA: Int([GrossPay]*0.062*100)/100** in the upper portion of the Expression Builder window. The **Int** function removes the fractional part of the number and returns the resulting integer value. This is necessary for our calculation here because we are multiplying **GrossPay** (a dollar amount) by a percentage and we want the result to be in dollars and cents. Click **OK** and click out of the **FICA** field.

FIGURE 6-27

26. Right-click on the **FICA** field and click on Properties. Click on Format and using the pull-down menu, change the Format to Currency.

27. Click on the Field property in the ninth column of the design grid and click on the Build icon in the menu bar. Type **Medicare: Int([GrossPay]*0.0145*100)/100** in the upper portion of the Expression Builder window. Click **OK** and click out of the **Medicare** field.

28. Right-click on the **Medicare** field and click on Properties. Click on Format and using the pull-down menu, change the Format to Currency.

29. Click on the Field property in the tenth column of the design grid and click on the Build icon in the menu bar. Double-click on **Tables** in the lower left portion of the window and click on the **Allowance Table**. Type **FIT: (([GrossPay]-** in the upper portion of the Expression Builder window. Double-click on **AllowanceAmount** in the middle of the lower portion of the Expression Builder window and click on the − (minus) symbol.

30. Click on the **Withholding Table** and double-click on **UpperLimit** in the middle of the lower portion of the Expression Builder window, click on the) (close parentheses) symbol, and click on the * (asterisk) symbol.

31. Double-click on **TaxRate** in the middle of the lower portion of the Expression Builder window, click on the) (close parentheses) symbol, click on the + (plus) symbol and double-click on **FWT** in the middle of the lower portion of the Expression Builder window. Click **OK**.

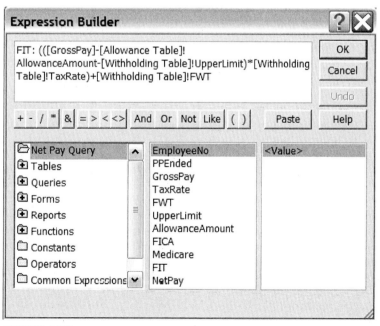

FIGURE 6-28

32. Click in the eleventh column of the design grid and type **NetPay: [GrossPay]-[FIT]-[FICA]-[Medicare]** in the Field property.

33. Before we run the query, we need to be sure that the formatting of the remaining fields is correct. Right-click on the **GrossPay** field and click on Properties. Click on Format and using the pull-down menu, change the Format to Currency. Do the same for the **FIT** and **NetPay** fields.

34. Click on the Run ! icon. Close and save the query as **Net Pay Query**.

KEY TERMS

union query

QUESTIONS AND PROBLEMS FOR REVIEW

MULTIPLE-CHOICE QUESTIONS

6.1 Tables in the payroll cycle can
  (a) Store reference data for use in calculating gross pay and payroll tax
  (b) Link employees and departments
  (c) Store payroll registers
  (d) Contain only one primary key
  (e) All of the above

6.2 The primary key for the Hours Worked Table should be:
  (a) The employee number
  (b) The department number
  (c) The employee number and the pay period
  (d) The employee number and the department number
  (e) None of the above

PROBLEMS

6.1 Dan Tragg has asked you to create a Payroll Register as of September 30, 2006.

6.2 Tragg's has also decided to print their Payroll checks and related earnings statements for their employees each period. Design this report. Create it so that it is one report that would result in the Payroll check being torn off the bottom for deposit in the bank. An example of this report is shown in Figure 6-29.

6.3 Query the system and find out how much Brenda Chan earned (net) as of September 30, 2006.

Earnings Statement

Tragg's Custom Surfboards
8713 Montauk Drive
La Selva Beach, CA 95076

Pay Period Ended

Pay Date: 9/30/2006

Employee No   1001
Dept No   10
Social Security No 630-30-3003

Dan W Tragg
8713 Montauk Place
La Selva Beach, CA 96076

Hours and Earnings					Taxes and Deductions		
Description	Hours	Rate	This Period	Year-To-Date	Description	This Period	Year-To-Date
Regular		$0.00	$0.00	$0.00	FICA:	$341.00	$341.00
Overtime		$0.00	$0.00	$0.00	Medicare:	$79.75	$79.75
Salary		$5,500.00	$5,500.00	$5,500.00	FIT:	$958.21	$958.21

Gross Pay Year To Date	Gross Pay This Period	Total Deductions This Period	Net Pay This Period
$5,500.00	$5,500.00	$1,378.96	$4,121.04

- -

Tragg's Custom Surfboards
8713 Montauk Drive
La Selva Beach, CA 95076

Pay Date: 9/30/2006

Pay to the
Order of ___Dan W Tragg_____

Pay
Amount: | $4,121.04 |

For _____   _____

FIGURE 6-29

INDEX